CAREER PLANNING

CAREER PLANNING

Third Edition

Dave Ellis

Stan Lankowitz

Ed Stupka

Doug Toft

Houghton Mifflin Company
Boston   New York

Senior Sponsoring Editor: Mary Finch
Associate Editor: Shani B. Fisher
Editorial Assistant: Andrew Sylvester
Senior Project Editor: Rachel D'Angelo Wimberly
Editorial Assistant: May Jawdat
Senior Production/Design Coordinator: Sarah L. Ambrose
Manufacturing Manager: Florence Cadran
Marketing Manager: Barbara LeBuhn
Senior Designer: Henry Rachlin

Cover credits: cover image © Stephen Gleason;
detail of an open book © Milton Montenegro/Getty
Images, Inc.; detail of an office clock © Steve
Cole/Getty Images, Inc.; pen pointing at an
electronic organizer © Janis Christie/Getty
Images, Inc.; laptop computer © Tony Stone Images;
Earth © Bruce Powell/Masterfile.

Photo Credits on page 122

Printed in the U.S.A.

ISBN: 0-618-23274-5

Notice: *Career Planning* was previously titled *Career Planning
Supplement to Becoming a Master Student.*

College Survival
A program of Houghton Mifflin Company
2075 Foxfield Road, Suite 100
St. Charles, IL 60174

CONTENTS

Introduction

X

Get the most from this book   1
What's in here?   2
This book might be wrong—and you can change that   5

CHAPTER 1

Commit

6

Career planning—enjoy the benefits   10
Think critically about career planning   12
Career planning—come as you are   14
If you want to be practical . . . dream   17
Tune up your conversation space   20
Quiz   23

CHAPTER 2

Discover Yourself   24

Discover who you *are*   25
One set of values   27
Discover your *learning styles*   29
Discover what you can *do*   33
Explore vocational assessments   36
Job skills for the new millennium   37
Discover what you *have*   39
Quiz   41

CHAPTER 3

Discover Work   42

You've got a world of choices   43
Learn more about the world of work   45
Test the waters—jump into the world of work   47
Gaining related experience—being an intern   50
Imagine a world without jobs   52
Connect to cyberspace   55
Finding what you want on the Internet   57
Make the information connection—using online resources in career planning   59
Thinking critically about information on the Internet   61
Return to the key player—YOU   63
Quiz   65

CHAPTER 4

Plan

66

If you want to be free, plan 67

7 ways to stop procrastination 69

Planning by creation 70

Four paths to more powerful goals 74

Fine-tune your career plan 76

Sample formats for career plans 78

Quiz 81

CHAPTER 5

Act

82

Use power tools for finding work 83

Tell everyone you know—the art of networking 87

Revitalize your résumé 89

Sample résumés 91

Sell your résumé with an effective cover letter 94

Sample cover letters 95

Use interviews to hire yourself an employer 97

Sample thank-you notes 100

Quiz 101

CHAPTER 6 Celebrate Work 102

Succeeding with coworkers—it's a matter of style   103

Join a diverse workplace   106

Dealing with sexism and sexual harassment   109

Practice "netiquette"   111

Forget your career   112

Sample life purposes   113

Some goals for the year 10,000   114

Celebrate mistakes   116

Celebrate your plan—then begin again   117

Keep your career plan alive   118

Quiz   120

Suggested Reading   121

Photo and Illustration Credits   122

Index   123

CAREER PLANNING

Introduction

For most people, the job market offers traps, blinds, false leads, and even mirages which block the way to their goals. Yet it offers countless rewarding opportunities for those who know their way around in it.
RICHARD LATHROP

All adventures, especially into new territory, are scary.
SALLY RIDE

AS YOU BEGIN . . . Consider one way to use this book to succeed in planning your career. Also do a textbook reconnaissance and discover options for getting the most from this book. You can declare what you want in planning your career and commit to making this book a partner in your success.

Get the most from this book

Any book is merely an invitation. Books invite you to think for yourself, come to terms with your dreams, and look at the world through new lenses. They invite you into the hearts, lives, and passions of other human beings. They invite you to plan, choose, create, reflect, and act.

This book invites you to practice planning your career. It distills many of the lessons people have learned while choosing careers and looking for work. If you apply the ideas in this book, you're likely to avoid dull, dead-end jobs. You might make more money. And you will probably save days, months, or even years or frustration in the work world.

This book does not guarantee those things. However, there is one thing it can guarantee. If you apply the ideas in this book, you will take charge of your career. You won't be leaving it to your boss, your teachers, the job market, a personnel department, or anyone else. You will be the author of your own life. You will choose how to live it.

Reading the articles in this book is an effective way to start planning your career. Even more powerful are reading and doing the book. That includes doing the exercises, answering quiz questions, and completing the Discovery Statements and Intention Statements, which are journal entries. Fill this book with your writing and keep plenty of extra paper on hand for recording more ideas. (Three-by-five index cards work especially well for this purpose; you can carry them in a pocket or purse, write on them, and sort them later.) Through taking action, you start putting ideas to work in your life.

You can read this book cover to cover, but you don't have to do that. Though the chapters are designed to be read in order, you can skip around and focus on the parts of the book that apply to your current situation. Look through the table of contents and the index to find what you want.

Without your active participation, this book is worthless. But if you combine reading with reflecting, dreaming, planning, writing, choosing, and acting, something will happen. You can get something in return for the money, effort, and time you put into this book. You can come away with a plan for what many people spend 88,000 hours of their lives doing: working. More than that, you could come away with a far greater chance to spend those hours doing work you choose, work that is worthy of your talents and dreams—work you love.

This book invites you to take charge of your career. It contains ideas, hints, suggestions, experiments, skills, resources, and tools. Only you can put them into action. If it sometimes seems overwhelming, take one suggestion at a time. Breaking a major project like career planning into small steps makes it doable. Building on a series of small successes, you can accomplish goals that do justice to your dreams.

All kinds of readers can use this book. It is for people beginning their careers, people well into their careers, people in career transition, people of various cultures and ethnic backgrounds—everyone.

You are invited to preview this book and discover what's in it for you.

What's in here?

You can use this book as a guide through six phases of activity: commit to career planning, discover yourself, discover the world of work, plan, act on your plan, and celebrate work. Key elements of this book promote these activities.

Discovery Statements help you learn more about your thought processes and what you think about your future career.

Intention Statements help you use what you have learned about career planning. In doing the **exercises**, you'll actually produce and evaluate ideas, thus gaining practical experience in career planning. A **web site** (**http://collegesurvival.college.hmco.com/students**) dedicated to this text offers additional articles, exercises, suggestions, ideas, and tools for expanding your career planning practices. Each chapter in this book has a specific purpose.

The main purpose of this introduction is to persuade you to commit to spending the energy to use this book actively. Before you stiffen up and resist, the purpose of this sales pitch is not to separate you from your money. You already bought the book. Now you can get something for your money by committing yourself to take action—in other words, commit yourself to planning your career. Here's what's in it for you.

Chapter One: Commit

Gives you an idea of what career planning involves. This includes a critical look at some common ideas about work and career planning. You can also take the opportunity to consider possible payoffs of career planning and decide how deeply you want to commit to this process. One step in creating your dream career is to dream. Finding work that you love means discovering what you love in the first place. This chapter asks you to let your imagination soar; dreaming is the foundation of a truly practical career plan.

Chapter Two: Discover Yourself

Is about an essential ingredient in every career plan: you. Your desires, preferences, interests, and abilities are a great place to start your career plan. Here you are asked to explore what you want to be, what you want to do, and what you want to have. You can start translating your skills and interests into careers you can plan.

Chapter Three: Discover Work

Discusses what's "out there" in the work world, another key to your career plan. Included are strategies for researching career options. With that knowledge, you can match your skills and interests with the opportunities that await you.

Chapter Four: Plan

Focuses on planning, a step that bridges dreams to reality. To some people, planning means getting locked into a rigid schedule, closing ourselves off from adventure, or losing the fun in life. Actually planning can put us more at ease and open us to change. By planning, we create new possibilities in every aspect of life. Planning creates freedom.

Chapter Five: Act

Asks you to put your career plan into action. This involves writing résumés, going on interviews, and more. Basing these steps on knowledge and planning empowers you in the job market.

Chapter Six: Celebrate Work

First invites you to think about the world of work by first finding success in getting along with your coworkers. Embrace diversity. Then celebrate—step back, laugh, relax, and remember the big picture. Recalling your broad goals and life purpose is part of this. So is beginning again, changing directions, and celebrating your mistakes.

Career planning boils down to expanding and narrowing down. Expanding involves opening up as many possibilities as you can, exploring whatever you're interested in, and surveying the full spectrum of available careers. If you choose a career too soon, you may not find out about a new field that holds the most promise for a career. You may miss learning about the company you never knew existed—the kind of place where you've always wanted to work. Or you might forget to consider self-employment, the chance to create your own business.

Narrowing down means choosing a field, focusing on certain skills to develop, and finding work. In career planning, there is a time to explore possibilities. There also comes a time to choose, to act. That calls for a pointed, specific plan.

The trick is to keep those two tasks in balance. Working through this book is one way to find a rhythm of expanding and narrowing down and move toward a career you love.

Action makes this book work. To get the most out of an exercise, read the instructions carefully before you begin. To get the most out of this book, do most of the exercises. These exercises invite you to write, touch, feel, move, see, search, ponder, speak, listen, recall, choose, commit and create. Learning often works best when it involves this action.

Remember, career planning is an adventure that involves exploration. There are dozens of effective paths to planning your career. This book will help you on your way.

JOURNAL ENTRY

Intention Statement

Even if you are not sure of your career preference, write a career plan right now. Include three elements: a career goal, a list of steps you can take to prepare for that career, and a timeline for reaching that career goal.

Your plan might be incomplete or tentative. No problem. This book will help you make it more complete. You can change this plan later—even throw it out and start over. Career planning is a continual cycle of discovery, intention and feedback. The point is to dive into the process and make career planning a lifelong habit.

You can plan now, with no further research. Go ahead. There's nothing to lose. Make an outline, do a mind map—use any format you like. Discover what you already know. Consider using your computer to complete this exercise.

EXERCISE

Cruise this book

When we encounter a landscape of new ideas, most of us learn best by first surveying the entire territory. For students, that means getting an overall sense of what a book or course is about before learning the specific details.

    With this in mind, take 15 minutes to skim this book. Go over each page quickly. Scan the headlines and bold print. Notice the illustrations, exercises, and journal entries.

    As you do this, you may already see ideas or techniques that look interesting. Note the page numbers and describe the ideas briefly.

Page Number   Description

This book might be wrong—
and you can change that

This book might be wrong. Some of the ideas in it may not work for you. Some of the exercises and journal entries may not take you where you expect to go. Some suggestions just may not apply to you right now. Exercises, journal entries, quizzes—it may all seem like too much.

Fortunately, there's a lot you can do about all this.

You can remember that ideas are tools.

Career planning is not a creed, formula, or dogma. It is not a recipe or painting by numbers. It is not a formal system, a schedule of obligations, or a list of requirements. There is nothing to sign and no hidden agenda.

In reality, career planning is only a body of ideas—tools—to try. You are not being called on to believe anything. You're only invited to test the techniques, try them on for size, and judge them for yourself. All of them have the goal of guiding you to a career that you choose freely and enjoy. If an idea or technique brings you closer to that goal, you can use it. If not, you can ignore it for now.

There is nothing mysterious about this. A career plan is merely a road map. It marks the high points of the trip, notes the landmarks, and tells us where to turn. Like a map, a career plan can save time and help us avoid getting lost.

A career plan is to life what a compass is to an explorer, or what a conductor is to an orchestra. Maps, compasses, conductors—none of these things are "true" or "false." Better words for describing them include *effective* or *ineffective, useful* or *not useful, accurate* or *inaccurate.*

Throughout this book, you may meet surprising ideas. Some of them may inspire anger or automatic rejection. For many people, the very idea of finding a dream career or enjoying work seems an illusion.

Another tendency is to grow attached to ideas. This is a very human tendency. Some ideas easily become our pets. We fasten on to them as the keys to the future. They even inspire our undying allegiance and become self-evident truths.

Readers with either attitude can squelch many of the benefits of career planning, even before they begin. An alternative is to release ourselves from these extremes.

In this process, there's no requirement to always be "right"—no plan, idea, or technique we must champion, attack, defend, or preserve. When we let go of those obligations, we may feel lighter, more detached, more playful. We glimpse possibilities we've never seen before. And with the blinders of a rigid position set aside, we can discover a career.

A note about gender-fair language
To avoid awkward sentence construction, the authors chose to alternate the use of male and female pronouns throughout this book. The intent is to use language that is as inclusive and bias-free as possible.

Commit

You must be the change you wish to see in the world.
MOHANDAS GANDHI

Instead of thinking about where you are, think about where you want to be. It takes twenty years of hard work to become an overnight success.
DIANA RANKIN

IN THIS CHAPTER . . . Begin now. Jump right into the process and write a career plan—now. Explore the choices you've already made. Discover what you already know and then find out more. Ask others about career planning. Begin to incorporate what you learned from doing these exercises—now.

What if I make the wrong choice?

You are not asked to make a final decision. You can always choose again. Changing your mind is OK. There is no right answer. You are exploring now. This is only practice.

What a strange way to start this book.

We learn by doing. This journal entry gets the process started. Later in the book, you'll be invited to do it again and notice your progress.

I don't know about my career yet!

That's OK, because the purpose of this assignment is just to begin the process of exploring.

I don't WANT to do this!

Examine your purpose for using this book. Forget the whole thing if it doesn't help you get what you want.

There's not enough room on the page for me to do this.

You can also use a notebook. You might want to use it for many of this book's other journal entries and exercises.

Begin now
JOURNAL ENTRY

Discovery/Intention Statement

Write your career plan.

Yes. Now.

Do this before you go any further in this book. Jump right into the process and discover what you already know about your wishes and plans for a career.

If you have no idea where to begin, make up something. This journal entry can get your started.

The plan you write right now might not match the reality of your future. That's not the point. A master, one who excels at an activity, fumbles when she first attempts her art. Even accomplished artists begin, revise, discard, and begin again. Ernest Hemingway rewrote the last page of *A Farewell to Arms* 39 times before he was satisfied.

What you are being asked to do is far less complicated. Just write a rough draft of your career plan on the following page. It's only for practice. At this point you can do nothing wrong. There are many opportunities to refine your plan as you use this book.

Your plan might take up one paragraph or one page. Or it might be longer, listing long-term and short-term goals. You might include a specific job title or list of tasks you enjoy. Or you could simply list the general values you'd like your work to support.

For example, one person's plan could include the steps necessary for becoming an anthropologist. It might list the courses required for this major and any additional training desired. Such a plan could also list tasks to do after schooling is complete. It might name companies to research, people to contact, and target dates for completing a résumé and interviews. This plan might take up several pages or a stack of 3×5 cards.

For other people, a much simpler plan may be appropriate. For now, this plan could be only one sentence long: "I will work as a music teacher in an elementary school." Or "On Monday I will contact the Career Planning Center and set up a time to talk with a counselor there."

To make your plan effective, make it visual. Put it in writing. If you prefer, use flow charts, mind maps, diagrams, or drawings. Some people like to list each action from their plan on a separate 3×5 card. To get the big picture, they pin the cards on a bulletin board or tape them to a wall.

The point is to get started with the process of planning—to make it a working tool in your life. As you experience the power of planning, you can return to it again and again.

When you write your plan, remember the difference between the terms *job* and *career*. In this book, *job* means a specific group of tasks, chores, or duties that make up whatever we call "work." A *career* is a general field of employment, a group of related jobs. Someone interested in the career of counseling, for example, could work in teaching, career counseling, social work, or the ministry.

To get started on your career plan, complete the following sentences:

1. The career I choose for now is …

2. The major steps that will guide me to this career are …

3. The immediate steps I will take to pursue this career are …

To complete this journal entry, begin writing now. Create your career plan in the space below.

_____

_____

_____

_____

_____

_____

_____

_____

_____

_____

_____

_____

JOURNAL ENTRY

Discovery Statement

Review the career plan you wrote in the previous journal entry. Does it reveal any career choices that you've already made? Does it reveal any issues you want to think about more?

List those choices or issues.

I discovered that I …

_____

_____

_____

_____

_____

_____

_____

If I write in my book and tear out some of the pages to show my instructor what I wrote, I will ruin my book.

Using the book actively will assist you in getting the most value out of it. If you just re-insert the page in the spine, it will hold. A piece of tape will hold it in place.

I really don't have any idea right now.

You might know more than you think. Just begin and see what happens. The only way to learn is to practice.

This will take too much time!

Plan however much time you think is appropriate and stick to your plan. Even 15 minutes can be very useful.

I'll wait until I've read more of the book before I do this.

Doing this now will help you get more out of the rest of the book. What you read will be more meaningful to you if you do this writing now.

I don't know how to begin or what to write.

Just dive in. Start writing anything that comes to your mind, even if it doesn't seem related. Experiment with this process.

EXERCISE

Discover what you know already

Before they begin career planning, many people know a lot about what they do not want to do for a living. Chances are you've already ruled out many jobs and careers, but this is not being negative—it can clarify the things you'd really like to do. At any time, you can choose a new list of careers and jobs you've ruled out for now. And you can be willing to reconsider your position later.

To do this exercise, scan the following lists, crossing out all the jobs you're not interested in.

1. Actuary, Chemist, Chiropractor, Dental Hygienist, Dentist, Dietitian, Electrocardiograph Technician, Forester, Geologist, Health Record Technician, Laboratory Technician, Licensed Practical Nurse, Mathematician, Medical Assistant, Meteorologist, Mining Engineer, Nuclear Engineer, Occupational Therapist. Optometrist, Pharmacist, Pharmacy Technician, Physical Therapist, Physical Therapy Assistant, Physicist, Podiatrist, Radiologist, Radiology Technician, Registered Nurse, Respiratory Therapist, Software Engineer, Stationary Engineer, Surgical Technician, Surveyor, Veterinarian, Water and Sewage Plant Operator.

2. Aerospace Engineer, Air Conditioning Mechanic, Air Traffic Controller, Aircraft Mechanic, Airline Pilot, Architect, Assembler, Automotive Mechanic, Boilermaker, Bookbinder, Broadcast Technician, Bus Driver, Carpenter, Chemical Engineer, Civil Engineer, Coin Machine Repairer, Computer Programmer, Computer Service Technician, Computer Software Designer, Computer Systems Analyst, Construction Inspector, Construction Machinery Operator, Construction Worker, Data Management Specialist, Diemaker, Electrical Engineer, Electrician, Electronics Technician, Industrial Engineer, Industrial Technologist, Landscape Architect, Laser Technician, Lithographer, Machine Tool Operator, Machinist, Mechanical Engineer, Metallurgical Engineer, Mining Engineer, Model Builder, Nuclear Engineer, Office Machine Repairer, Optician, Painter, Petroleum Engineer, Photoengraver, Pipe Fitter, Plumber, Printing Press Operator, Refrigeration Mechanic, Sheet Metal Worker, Telephone Installer, Telephone Repairer, Toolmaker, Truck Driver, TV Mechanic, Web Programmer, Welder.

3. Accountant, Administrative Assistant, Auditor, Bank Manager, Bank Officer, Bank Teller, Bookkeeper, Buyer, Cashier, Certified Public Accountant, Clerk Typist, Commodity Buyer, Court Reporter, Economist, Food Service Manager, Hospital Administrator, Hotel Manager, Insurance Agent, Insurance Underwriter, Labor Relations Specialist, Manufacturer's Sales Representative, Marketing Manager, Office Administrator, Park Administrator, Personnel Specialist, Production Manager, Public Administrator, Public Relations Specialist, Purchasing Agent, Real Estate Agent, Receptionist, Retail Buyer, Sales Manager, Secretary, Securities Sales Worker, Transportation Planner, Word Processor.

4. Actor, Architect, Artist, Commercial Artist, Computer Analyst, Dancer, Designer, Editor, Fashion Designer, Graphic Artist, Interior Decorator, Interior Designer, Jeweler, Model Builder, Musician, Newscaster, Pattern Maker, Photographer, Radio/TV Announcer, Reporter, Singer, Technical Illustrator, Writer.

5. Automotive Body Repair Technician, Automotive Mechanic, Barber, Bartender, Carpenter, Computer Trainer, Cook, Corrections Officer, Cosmetologist, Counselor, Dental Assistant, Dental Hygienist, Fashion Merchandiser, Firefighter, Flight Attendant, Guard, Lawyer, Legal Assistant, Librarian, Library Technician, Minister, Nursery School Educator, Nursing Assistant, Park Manager, Police Officer, Priest, Psychologist, Rabbi, Reservations Agent, School Administrator, Social Worker, Sociologist, Solar Technician, Teacher, Teacher's Aide, Travel Agent, Urban Planner, Waiter.

Next, go through the five lists again and circle the jobs that sound interesting to you. Finally, from the jobs you circled, choose the three that interest you the most and write them here.

_____

_____

JOURNAL ENTRY

Intention Statement

Write an Intention Statement describing how you will find out more about the three jobs you chose at the end of the previous exercise.

Career planning—
enjoy the benefits

Career planning is a relatively new field. Throughout history, many people simply mirrored their parents' choice of career. Women became housewives, teachers, or nurses. Men went into farming or business. Today that's changed.

Even so, career planning is often unknown or untried. It is common for people to spend less than 20 hours in a lifetime on career planning. That's less time than many of them spend watching television in one week.

Career planning involves adventure and exploration. It can transform the experience of working from repetitive drudgery into playful excitement. That can happen in several ways, and each amounts to a sales pitch for career planning.

Pitch #1: Choose in the face of constant change

In our country, the numbers and types of jobs are growing fast. Thirty years ago, there were few jobs for applications programmers, systems analysts, or robot repair technicians. When looking over lists of available jobs, people rarely saw openings for hazardous waste managers, video text designers, laser technicians, or genetic engineers. Even 15 years ago, few considered becoming geriatric social workers, VCR technicians, full-time day care providers, or cable TV producers.

In addition to constantly adding new jobs, our economy is phasing our others. Careers pursued by thousands of people today may no longer exist in 10 years.

The rate of change in many fields is accelerating. This is especially true of the computer industry, where the life span of the latest technology is measured in months. Without constant updating, sales and technical people would be hopelessly lost.

Each year nearly 40 million Americans change jobs. Many workers will go through three to six career changes during a lifetime. Not just job changes—career changes.

Viewed this way, career planning becomes less of a luxury. Instead, it can be a tool for keeping your head in a complex and constantly changing future.

Pitch #2: Move from chance to choice

Many people never have the experience of choosing their work. Instead, work choose them. Driven by desperation or chance, they take the first job that comes along—one that has little to do with their interests. One experience of leaving jobs to chance can set up a lifelong pattern.

Career planning is about choice. In this process, we discover the full scope of our abilities. We learn that our society offers a limitless range of jobs. We find that our favorite activities help us develop valued skills, and we encounter proven techniques for job hunting. Each of these facts multiplies our options. They increase the odds that our careers will stay in line with our dreams.

To get what you want out of your career, begin with your dreams. Know what you want. Before you make your goals clear to an employer, first make them clear to yourself.

PITCH #3: *Go where you want to go*

Learning by trial and error works well with some subjects. An error in career direction, though, carries some major costs. It could mean weeks, months, or years in a job with little challenge. It might mean failing to even hear about the career that would have been just right. Years of retraining or reschooling, losing hundreds or thousands of dollars in income, getting laid off or fired—these are potential costs, too.

None of these experiences mean the end of the world. In fact, we can learn powerful lessons from them. It's also possible to find a career in ways that are less painful and more joyful.

All it takes is asking: What if? What if I choose this career? Would I enjoy this work? What would I do in my job every day? Would this job relate to anything I care about? Is it consistent with what I want out of life? What do I want out of life anyway?

Such questions are liberating. They cut down on blind guesses and invest our lives with purpose, meaning, and direction.

PITCH #4: *Learn to plan*

We can apply planning skills across many activities— completing a term paper, meeting a deadline at work, saving money, or buying a car. Planning can help us in losing weight, quitting smoking, or learning to play the guitar; in deciding whether to take calculus or major in English. In fact, planning is one skill that enhances almost anything else we do.

PITCH #5: *Get more out of the present*

Career planning is not about something that takes place in the hazy, distant future. It's about making smart choices right now. A career direction helps you choose what school to attend and which courses to take. Your career choice influences whom you meet, what you read, where you live, what you wear, what you eat, how much exercise you get, how you spend your time, and how satisfied you feel with your life. Career planning is about choices you'll make in the next day, the next hour—the next five minutes.

PITCH #6: *You're planning a career anyway*

It is impossible to avoid career planning. Even the decision not to plan is a kind of plan. It's often the same as saying, "My plan is to just let things work out for themselves" or "I'll think about careers later."

We often make decisions about what courses to take, where to look for work, and which skills to develop. All of these affect our future work, even if we don't label them "career planning." When you commit to career planning, you can make these decisions with more skill.

EXERCISE

Ask other people about career planning

Ask three people you think are successful in their careers how much time they spent planning their futures. Also ask how they went about planning their careers and if they see any benefits in doing so. List their key ideas below.

_____

_____

_____

_____

_____

_____

_____

_____

_____

_____

_____

_____

JOURNAL ENTRY

Discovery/Intention Statement

Write about how you will apply any of your insights from the above exercise to your own career plan.

I intend to …

_____

_____

_____

_____

_____

_____

Think critically about

Traditional beliefs about career planning often include certain ideas:

1 I don't know where to start.

2 The best way to plan a career is to enter a field that is in demand.

3 All the planning in the world won't change the number and kinds of jobs available.

4 I don't have any work experience, so I don't have any skills.

5 With school, work, and family I'm already overextended. I don't have the interest, time, or energy for career planning.

6 I know what I want to do. Why should I waste my time on career planning?

7 I'm in school now, so I don't have to worry about career planning until the future.

These ideas, even when we are not aware of them, can color our actions. With such attitudes, it's no wonder that some people find career planning as enjoyable as chicken pox.

To generate new possibilities for career planning, consider alternatives. One sure-fire way is to put a positive slant on the opposite point of view and assign yourself a proactive role. Like most of the important challenges in life, this requires an open mind, critical thinking, and commitment to get involved. Below are the opposite of the ideas state above, reworded in a positive, proactive way.

1

This book can help you get started.

Career planning is a many faceted, open-ended process that will help you learn more about yourself and the world of work. There is no one "right way" to begin. This book will introduce you to ideas, strategies, and tools that can dramatically change the way you see yourself and life in general. It will get you started on the lifelong journey of planning for the future. It can give you confidence to explore and initiate new and challenging options you never considered before.

Success in career planning does not depend on specialized knowledge or training. It rests on a commitment to learn, to plan and then to act on what you know. That commitment is something only you can provide.

2

It's practical to enter a field I enjoy—even if it's not in demand.

When planning careers, we may be tempted to choose fields with the most job openings. This could work against our long-term goals. Even in fields that are highly competitive, there are usually openings for qualified people. And jobs that are "hot" today may be "cool" by the time you've completed your education. In the fact of accelerating change, your own interests and values can be just as reliable as current trends.

Some people limit their careers to the job titles displayed most prominently in the want ads. By doing so, they may overlook their own genuine interests and abilities. In addition, only a fraction of the available job openings may be advertised there—as few as 20 percent.

3

Planning will help you take charge of your future.

Although it is a choice, you don't have to settle for whatever career happens to come along. Career planning is not simply choosing the "right" career but involves increasing your knowledge, seeing new possibilities, and taking action to create a satisfying and rewarding career. This book can help you take charge of your future. Applying what you learn can maximize the career options available to you. Becoming the director of career planning in your life does not automatically insulate you from all the ups and downs of life, but it can smooth out the bumps and make the journey a lot more enjoyable.

4

With or without formal work experience, I have skills.

It's easy to fall prey to the fallacy "I don't have a skill unless someone has paid me to use it full-time." People constantly use skills for which they receive little or no money. Some choose to stay home and care for their families full-time. They plan and prepare meals, coordinate health care and education for their children, and manage household finances. These are true work skills.

Students also gain skills, even if they don't work. Students write, manage research projects, speak in public, and think

career planning

critically. They also take part in internships, cooperative education programs, and volunteer work.

Word processing, driving cars, drawing, playing sports, cutting hair, evaluating movies, organizing closets, telling jokes—these and a thousand other common activities develop skills that employers will pay for.

5

Even if you feel overextended, there is no better time to begin planning your future than now.

When it comes to career planning, sooner is better than later. It is the best of all options when you begin taking an active role in shaping your career right from the start. A little planning now can save you a lot of heartaches in the future. It will enable you to improve your skills, increase your knowledge, and enhance your decision making. Many of life's disappointments can be avoided if you invest the time and effort needed to explore your options sooner rather than putting it off until later.

6

Approach career planning as though you don't know what you want to do.

Career planning can reinforce the decisions already made or, if done with an open mind, it can introduce you to possibilities that you overlooked or were not aware of. Think of it as an insurance policy with two payoffs. It can either give you peace of mind to understand clearly why you made the choices you did or help you see new possibilities that you had never considered before.

7

I'm in school, so I can start planning my career now.

A course in French suddenly takes on new meaning when your goal is to work in a foreign embassy. A required writing course seems like an opportunity once you've decided to become a magazine editor or newspaper reporter. Career planning can make a difference for the work you're doing in school now. And whenever you can relate course work to a personal goal, you tape a limitless source of energy.

EXERCISE

Generate new ideas for career planning

Here's a chance to practice the art of creating options. Restate each of the following ideas by putting a positive slant on the opposite point of view and assigning yourself a proactive role in implementing the idea.

Career planning is only for people who are undecided about their careers

_____
_____
_____
_____

Writing a career plan now means it will be a hassle to change it later.

_____
_____
_____
_____

When the job market is tight, there are fewer career options for me.

_____
_____
_____
_____

I can't plan a career now. I can't afford to take the time from my schoolwork.

_____
_____
_____
_____

Career planning—
come as you are

People put off career planning for a host of reasons. Some of the most common include:

- It will all work out for the best anyway.
- Others seem to handle it fine without all that work.
- It takes too much time.
- I'm just trying to make it through school.
- I don't need to worry about this right now.
- All I need to do is send in my résumé and answer the want ads.
- Career planning is kind of fun, but it's a pie-in-the-sky exercise.
- I already know what I want to do.
- This is not the right time.
- It's silly to even start thinking about careers right now.

Understand that planning for your career is part of college

Higher education presents you with many choices—where to attend school, how to structure your time, what to study and with whom to associate. You will find that this experience is valuable practice when you make the move from college to career. While there may not be tests when you're on the job, the grading might be tougher. Your boss may expect more from you than some of your professors.

Your commitment in college is good practice for making the transition to career. Build support systems into your life by cultivating new friendships, including those with members of other races and cultures. School activities, student services, volunteering and study groups are places to find support. Student services include career planning and placement, counseling services, financial aid, student ombudspersons, language clubs, and programs for minority students.

Focus on the process

One possibility in planning for your career is to come as you are. Take the first step in career planning from where you stand now—wherever that is. At this point it's the process that matters, not the results.

This book is based on the idea that you have a choice. You can make a plan. You can chart your way. There is possibility, promise, and passion in the world of work. You can find work that expresses your values and draws on your skills. Your career can build on your interests and actually give you more energy than it takes. You can find work that supports your life purpose. You can even look forward to Monday mornings: *You are on the edge of a universe so miraculous and full of wonder that your imagination at its most creative moment cannot encompass it. Paths are open to lead you to worlds beyond your wildest dreams.*

You can apply this to your career. Making it happen starts with commitment.

Some meanings of commitment

Committing yourself to career planning means a lot of things. It means dreaming about the life and work that excite you most.

Commitment to career planning means discovering how to create those moments again in the work you do every day. It means dreaming, relishing, remembering, getting excited. It means trying on new ideas and new roles. It also means choosing a new path, if that's appropriate.

Commitment to planning a career means analyzing, choosing, writing, and coming to terms with the work world. It means making contacts. It implies the freedom to be wrong, to forgive yourself, to explore, and to change your mind. Most of all, this commitment means a never-ending cycle of choosing, discovering, and starting over.

If you really use this book, you'll do all these things. It can be hard work. And if you accept the reports of many students who try career planning, it can be fun and rewarding too.

This book is about taking charge of your career—and along with it, your life. It's about becoming a master planner. It's about keeping disappointment, lost dreams, sadness, and regret to a minimum. Career planning is about the freedom to work with passion, energy, enthusiasm, and even joy.

If you're skeptical, read on. Play with the strategies outlined in this book. Then judge for yourself.

Commit to career planning

Take this opportunity to get your money's worth from this book. Circle the statement that represents your level of commitment:

1. "Well, I bought the book, didn't I?"

2. "I'll skim the book and see if anything looks worthwhile."

3. "I'll read the whole book and work at remembering the main ideas."

4. "I'll study this book and do some of the exercises and journal entries."

5. "I'll master this book, fill it with my writing, and constantly be on the lookout for any tool that will help me find the career I want."

If you circled statement 1, you may have wasted your money. See if you can get it back. If you chose statement 5, you're on the way to a fulfilling career. And if you fell somewhere in between, use this book for a while and see if it works for you. If it does, consider raising your level of commitment.

 Imagine for a moment that you had enough money to sustain yourself for a lifetime. Visit the Houghton Mifflin Career Planning web site and access the **Now that you've got money handled** exercise at http://collegesurvival.college. hmco.com/students. Work through the exercise by brainstorming about your goals and moving towards achieving them.

JOURNAL ENTRY

Discovery Statement

Imagine the course of your life assuming that you will do no career planning. You'll think about careers only when you're unhappy with your current job. Taking this approach, consider what work you might end up doing. Do you foresee any outcomes you would like to avoid?

    Without career planning, I can see myself . . .

_____

_____

_____

_____

_____

_____

_____

_____

Next, do a very general career plan. What work would you like to be doing in 5, 10, and 20 years? Quickly list four or five steps for reaching those career goals.

_____

_____

_____

_____

_____

_____

_____

_____

Now think about the advantages and disadvantages of the planned and the unplanned approaches. Does one approach offer more benefits? Does one offer a greater chance of finding work that you enjoy and value? Could one approach result in a more satisfying life? Could one approach save time or money? Write about the benefits and costs of each approach.

_____

_____

_____

_____

_____

_____

_____

If you want to be practical . . . dream

Career planning does not begin with grinding out résumés, churning out cover letters, poring over want ads, saving for an MBA, or completing a 200-question vocational interest test. Rather, it begins with wishing, reflecting, contemplating, imagining, pondering, savoring, and relishing. Career planning starts with your dream.

Dreaming makes sense in a hard-nosed, practical way. Consider people who change careers in mid-life. Often they talk about the need for work that fulfills them. Many of them have been in the work force for several decades. They've raised families, taken out mortgages, gone into debt, bought life insurance, and acquired possessions. They've spent a lifetime being "practical."

When such people decide to change careers, they're frequently looking for more than just another job. Instead, they speak of discovering a meaning and purpose in life. At the center of that quest is work that not only pays the bills but excites their passion and enthusiasm.

Instead of waiting 10, 20, or 30 years to discover your passions, you can begin now. This does not mean slighting the other tasks often associated with career planning—defining interests, listing skills, writing résumés, filling out applications, going on interviews. It only means that such tasks come later in the process.

When the subject of careers comes up, some people advise us to "just accept whatever happens with work. Even if you hate your job, you can do whatever you want in your free time." Consider that all your time is free time. There is no work you have to do. There is no attitude you have to hold. Our jobs follow directly from the plans and decisions we make. All of us are "self-employed," even when we work full-time for someone else. We give our time and skills to an employer or a client, and we do this for our own purposes.

In order to find work you enjoy, first discover exactly what it is you enjoy. Explore your dreams. Consider what you want in your career—and in every other area of your life. Such activity is not a meaningless or idle exercise. It's an investment in your future. The following exercise and journal entry can help guide you to that discovery.

EXERCISE

JOURNAL ENTRY

Imagine your ideal life

On a separate sheet of paper, write a free-form fantasy about your "perfect" life. What would you do if you had no money worries and all the free time you wanted? What would one day in this life be like? Where would you live? Who would be with you? When would you get up? What would you do each hour of the day?

Describe your daily routine, lifestyle, relationships, use of time, possessions, income, and geographical location. In your mind, see yourself actually doing the things you'd love to do each day.

Stay in the present tense. Write quickly and keep your pen moving. Don't worry about grammar, punctuation, or spelling. You may even want to jot down just phrases, single words, or random images. If you want, draw pictures or diagrams to capture what's in your mind.

Most people find it works best to just register first impressions. These can be significant. Trying to fit your ideal life into existing jobs, careers, lifestyles, locations, or companies is too limiting at this point. Yes, this might seem unrealistic and difficult. Try it anyway. The purpose is self-discovery—not immediate action.

When doing this exercise, be outrageous. Push your ideas of what's possible to the limits.

Discovery/Intention Statement

Imagine you're a reporter writing a feature story for one of your favorite magazines. Play the part of that reporter and write about yourself 20 years from today. Answer these questions:

What are the highlights of the past 20 years in your career and personal life?

_____

_____

_____

_____

_____

_____

What was your most important accomplishment in the past 20 years?

_____

_____

_____

_____

_____

_____

What would you tell someone who's entering your field of work?

_____

_____

_____

_____

_____

_____

What are your major career goals for the next 20 years?

_____

_____

_____

_____

_____

_____

_____

EXERCISE

Write your own definition of success

The slick pages in popular magazines scream out a hundred definitions of success. They glorify fat bank accounts, fan clubs, yachts, limousines, and chauffeurs. You'll see carpeted offices, teakwood desks that take up half a conference room, executive suites, and private secretaries. Other images of success include having a face that everyone recognizes, a company named after you, a twenty-room house with three fireplaces, and a wardrobe that fills seven closets.

Some people laugh off these plush images. Others simply accept popular definitions of success without much thought. In planning a career, it's useful to go one more step and define what success means to you.

To start thinking about success, glance through a popular magazine at a library or a bookstore. Then complete this sentence:

As judged by the articles and ads in this magazine, success is …

_____

_____

_____

Do the same with a popular TV show or the commercials aired during that show.

These presentations suggest that …

_____

_____

_____

Would these definitions of success and the good life promote your own career plans and values? How does your notion of success compare to those promoted by the mass media? Complete the following sentence:

To me, success means …

_____

_____

_____

_____

EXERCISE

Do your dream career now

Imagine that the people closest to you—family, friends, coworkers—are now suddenly enlightened. They will give you unconditional support, both emotional and financial, to do whatever you choose.

As of today, you also possess whatever skills you want to achieve your career goals. If you're a "wanna be" rock star even though you can't carry a tune, *voilà*! You now possess a thunderous, stunning voice. If you always wanted to be a surgeon but never wanted to invest in the necessary training, no problem. You are now a surgeon on a par with the greatest in the world.

Look to see if any other constraints in your life prevent you from doing what you want to do. This could be anything that you see as a limitation: your size, gender, race, nationality, physical ability, and so on. Simply imagine that these limits no longer exist. Don't worry about *how* to make this happen. Just play with the possibilities.

In short, you now have the skills, support, time, and money to do whatever you want. Now describe the career you would choose. Write on a separate sheet of paper.

When you've finished writing, consider whether your response suggests any possible goals for your future. Ask: What's interesting to me about this career? Could I make this interest part of my life *without* retraining or even making it a career? (For example, the person who loves to sing could join a church choir without becoming a professional musician.) Record your answers as goals on 3×5 cards.

Tune up your conversation space

Career planning is largely about introducing a new conversation into your life. In a sense, planning your career amounts to tuning up your conversation space.

If the term *conversation space* is new to you, don't be surprised. It's not in the dictionary. Even so, this term points to a practice that can reshape your relationships, your work, and your very experience of time.

Here the word *conversation* includes any occurrence of thinking, speaking, writing, listening, watching, or reading. Talking with another person face-to-face is one type of conversation. Watching television is also a way of taking part in a conversation, even if it seems one-sided. Other examples of conversation are reading the newspaper, writing an article, listening to the radio, going to a meeting, or making an entry in a personal journal.

All these activities involve both exposure to information and ideas and your reactions to them. When combined, these activities take up a lot of "space" in our lives. That is, they make up a lot of what we do.

Moment by moment, we choose ways to fill our conversation space. Minute by minute, we make choices about where to place our attention. Every second presents us with an opportunity to choose our conversations—what we listen to, talk about, watch, read, and therefore think about.

Conversations can be described in dozens of ways. For the purposes of this book, we can classify conversations according to their focus in time. At any moment, we can ask: Where is my conversation resting right now—past, present, or future?

Focus on the past

Most people fill their conversation space with the past. They focus on events that took place five minutes, five weeks, five years, or even five decades ago. The same can be said of our media. Most television programs, radio shows, newspapers, and magazines dwell on events of the past. This is not good, not bad—just typical.

Focus on the present

There is a second way that we can fill our conversation space—focusing on the present. This is the domain of artistry, excellence, and joy. This is the focus of the tennis player at the moment of a great swing, the musician giving a great performance, the mountain climber ascending a sheer cliff. Friendship, romance, good meals, massage, and sex also offer opportunities to savor the present moment.

Focus on the future

Another option is to fill our conversation space with the future. This is the time we spend thinking, writing, reading, listening, and speaking about what's yet to come in our lives, including our careers.

For many of us, conversations about the future usually focus on prediction. This happens even in sophisticated think tanks. Here conversations typically dwell on forecasting—in a word, prediction. Talk is seldom about the future that people want. Instead, conversation is about the kind of future they will have *if present trends continue.* The resulting predictions about the future of our education, society, or planet often lead people to worry.

When worry and prediction dominate our future, we find little space for creating a future that we want. In fact, worrying and talking about the past can become a kind of addiction that chokes off other possibilities.

We can draw a diagram that represents our conversation space and how much of it is typically devoted to the past, present, and future. For many of us, that diagram would look like this:

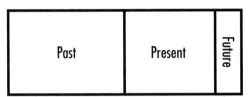

Find balance

From reading thus far, you might get the idea that speaking about the past is bad, while speaking about the future is good. Actually, conversations about the past can

be wonderful, affirming, and powerful. This is how many of us relax, celebrate, learn, and deepen our relationships. There also is no problem with prediction. At times, prediction is appropriate and even necessary for survival.

The point is that we can have all the options. One benefit of creating the future is the opportunity to balance our conversations among the past, present, and future. When that happens, our overall conversation space looks like this:

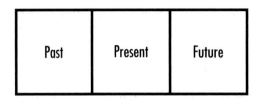

The suggestion here is to continue having conversations about the past and the present. Then *round out your conversation space by creating the future.* Talk about the career you *want* to have, the future you *choose* to create. Instead of predicting the future and extrapolating from current trends, start changing the trends.

It's not useful to limit conversations to any one period of time, just as it's not useful to eat only one food. Creating the future allows us to become trilingual—equally skilled at speaking about the past, the present, and the future we want to create.

Discovery/Intention Statement

One way to balance your conversation space is to devote approximately equal time to the past, the present, and the future—about 33 percent for each. This is only one option for filling your conversation space. You could also choose to devote 50 percent of your conversations to the present, or only 10 percent of conversations to the past and 40 percent to the future. Many other combinations are possible.

Describe the kind of balance *you* want as you choose the focus of your conversations and plan your career. If you like, represent your plan visually.

I intend to …

_____

_____

_____

_____

_____

Just open your mouth and speak your future

Sometimes we don't know what we want to say until we literally open our mouths and speak it. Powerful goals can emerge from daring, reckless verbal creation. What's more, speaking can turn a general goal into a specific one, an abstract goal into a concrete one.

Writing down a goal is one way to make it come alive. Speaking about a goal gives it yet another dimension of life. When you speak a goal, it resonates with your voice, your very breath.

Practice speaking your goals in the presence of another person who will be your partner for this exercise. Ask that person to function as a sympathetic listener—one who will not interrupt as you speak, ask questions, or criticize any of your goals. Also ask this person to record your goals on 3x5 cards.

Once you've created a sate atmosphere, just speak. Talk about your goals without rehearsing or editing your thoughts. These goals can relate to your career or any other aspect of your future.

The point is this: Just speak even before you know what to say—and listen to what comes out of your mouth. You can begin by saying, "What I want is …." or "What I *might* do is …." Another option is to say, "I've got several brand-new goals I've never spoken to anyone before. The first goal is …." Then finish any of these sentences with as many ideas as you can create.

Speak your goals for five minutes. Then switch roles and let the other person speak her goals for five minutes while you listen.

As you do this exercise, keep the following ideas in mind:

- Quality is not an issue. Remember that you don't have to adopt or act on any of the goals that you speak.

- Prepare for something wonderful and unexpected to happen. You might speak a goal that's never occurred to you before. You might create a plan that seems so on-track that you'll want to make it part of your life right away.

- Maintain an environment of safety. Let your partner "try on" outrageous plans without the fear of being quoted in public. Keep what you hear confidential. Listening with full, permissive attention to another person's wishes for the future is an empowering and unusual gift.

- If you feel any signs of fear or apprehension about what you'll say, just notice these feelings. Then continue speaking your goals. When in doubt, just keep your lips moving.

- If you get stuck during this exercise, read off or recall a few goals you've written before.

- Stand up as you speak your goals. Many of us think better on our feet.

- As you speak, allow completely new goals—no preconceptions, no agendas, no limits. Don't worry about telling the other person what he or she wants to hear. Simply speak your greatness.

Do this exercise regularly, with people you know well and those you know hardly at all. Gradually lengthen the amount of time you spend speaking goals. Go from 5 minutes to 10 minutes, 15, and even 20 or more.

Name _____ Date _____/_____/_____

1 When can you begin planning your career? Explain your answer.

2 What does commitment to career planning mean to you?

3 List three alternatives to your first thoughts about career planning.

4 Dreams and wishes are fun, but they are not useful when it comes to serious career planning. True or False? Explain your answer.

5 How can you change your conversation space to make it a more effective place for career planning?

Discover Yourself

> Some of the best lessons we ever learn are learned from past mistakes. The error of the past is wisdom and success of the future.
>
> DR. DALE E. TURNER

> New opportunities await and abound. Never stagnate and settle.
>
> KATHERINE NEGERMAJIAN

IN THIS CHAPTER . . . Discover who you are. Consider your values. Reflect on your personal qualities. Discover your *learning styles*. Think about your role models and how they influence your views and values. Commit to developing new skills and competencies.

Discover who you _are_

At an early age, many of us encountered the question "What do you want to be when you grow up?" Common answers to this everyday question bring up ideas worth examining.

Someone asks, "What do you want to be?" One response is to name a job. "I want to be an accountant or a manager of finance for a large company." Or "I want to be a doctor or teacher." These answers really suggest what we want to do.

Another response is to describe a certain income level or lifestyle. "I'd like to be rich, with all the free time in the world." Or "I want to have only a few possessions. That way I'll be free to pack up all my belongings at any time and move to Hawaii." Such statements actually reveal what we'd like to have.

Describing what we want to do and what we'd like to have are important. Yet neither of them is a complete answer to the question "What do you want to be?" Instead of naming a career or listing possessions, we could describe the personal qualities and values we bring to any job or lifestyle.

This suggests new answers to the query "What do you want to be?" Those answers might include being reliable, trustworthy, responsible for our lives, dependable, lovable, creative, patient, involved, honest, productive, self-defining, and accountable. These are just a few examples of personal values.

Often it's subtle messages about our values that influence what we have and do. The person who celebrates her abilities and fully expects to live a rewarding life will find a fulfilling career. And the person who's convinced that she's unlovable may never find work she enjoys.

So if you want it, be it. If you value being a successful student, live with the idea that you already are one. If you value satisfying work, live with the idea that you have many choices and are on the way to a successful career.

The exercises and journal entries in this chapter will help you explore your preferred ways of being.

EXERCISE

Clarify your values

This exercise provides you with a chance to clarify your commitment to various values. This is not a time to consider specific, attainable goals (things to have or do) but rather a time to reflect on more fundamental decisions about who you are and who you want to be. For example, you might commit to being loving, patient, accountable for your actions, or forgiving.

Complete the sentences below.

I am committed to being …

_____

_____

_____

This means …

_____

_____

_____

I am committed to being …

_____

_____

_____

This means …

_____

_____

_____

I am committed to being …

_____

_____

_____

This means …

_____

_____

_____

Next, use a dictionary to look up the three key descriptive words you have just written and find synonyms that might further develop or more accurately define your values.

After studying what you have just written, take a sheet of paper and list your values. Then define them with words that will remind you of who you intend to be. For ideas and suggestions, read the following article titled "One set of values."

Consider your own statement of values to be a living document. Revisit it periodically as you gain more insight and experience.

One set of values

As you clarify your values and apply them to career choices, review this list of examples for ideas.

Value: Be accountable

This means being:

- Honest
- Reliable
- Trustworthy
- Dependable
- Responsible

Being accountable includes making and keeping agreements—operating with integrity.

Value: Be loving

This means being:

- Affectionate
- Dedicated
- Devoted
- Equitable
- Accepting

Being loving includes appreciating ourselves and others—being gentle, considerate, forgiving, respectful, friendly, and courteous. It also includes being nonantagonistic, nonresistant, inclusive, understanding, compassionate, fair, and ethical.

Value: Be self-generating

This means being:

- Self-responsible
- The creator of our internal experiences—regardless of our external circumstances

Being self-generating includes not being a victim and not blaming others. Instead, we choose how to interpret and respond to all stimuli.

Value: Be promotive

This means being:

- Nurturing
- Contributing—charitable; thrifty; generous with time, money, and possessions

- Frugal—achieving the best results with the fewest possible dollars
- Helpful
- Encouraging
- Reasonable
- Judicious
- Cooperative—working as a member of a team or a community
- Appreciative

Value: Be candid

This means being:

- Honest
- Authentic
- Genuine
- Self-expressed
- Frank
- Outspoken
- Spontaneous
- Sincere
- Free of deceit
- Able to avoid false modesty without arrogance
- Self-disclosing
- Open about strengths and weaknesses

Value: Be detached

This means being:

- Impartial
- Unbiased
- Experimental
- Satisfied
- Patient (not resigned)
- Open-minded
- Without distress
- Adaptable
- Trusting
- Tolerant
- Willing to surrender
- Joyful—fun-loving, humorous, lighthearted, and happy

Detachment includes being separate from but aware of thoughts, emotions, body, health, accomplishments, relationships, desires, commitments, possessions, values, opinions, roles, and expectations. The opposite of detachment is being addicted (physically or emotionally), dogmatic, bigoted, absolutely certain, prejudiced, anxious, grave, or somber.

Value: Be aware of the possible

This means being:

- Creative
- Imaginative
- Resourceful
- Inventive
- Foresighted
- Holistic
- Visonary
- Inquisitive
- Audacious
- Exploring

Being aware of the possible means expecting great things of ourselves and others.

Value: Be involved

This means being:

- Committed
- Participative
- Focused—precise and attentive to detail
- Enthusiastic—having intense or eager interest
- Enduring—persistent, persevering
- Courageous—vulnerable, willing to take risks, trusting
- Energetic—displaying the capacity for action or accomplishment; being vigorous, robust, hardy, rugged, and strong
- Productive—putting ourselves at risk, operating with something at stake, pursuing excellence, acting with a sense of urgency yet without panic, and allowing projects to matter

JOURNAL ENTRY

JOURNAL ENTRY

Discovery Statement

Look for the enduring themes in your life—the activities that persist over time. For example, you might recall that you've worked in a restaurant each summer for the past three years. What did you enjoy about that activity? Was it preparing food, contact with people, or a flexible schedule? Write such reflections.

I enjoyed ...

_____

_____

_____

_____

_____

_____

_____

_____

_____

_____

Next, write about the personal qualities developed by this job or life experience: What kind of person did you become? More patient? Flexible? Organized? Efficient? Then ask if any of these answers are relevant to your career choice.

_____

_____

_____

_____

_____

_____

_____

_____

_____

_____

_____

_____

_____

_____

Discovery Statement

Remember a time when you felt powerful and competent. Examples might include writing a paper when the words flowed effortlessly, skillfully leading a bar mitzvah service, or making a long shot in a basketball game.

Re-create this experience as you write about it in detail on a separate sheet of paper. Remember all the sights, sounds, feelings, tastes, and smells. Exaggerate and heighten the glory of the moment. List the activities you were performing at that moment and any skills you used. What values were you living at that moment?

Reflect on any lasting changes in your outlook or behavior following the experience. Are any of them relevant to your career plan?

_____

_____

_____

_____

_____

_____

_____

_____

_____

_____

_____

_____

_____

_____

_____

_____

_____

_____

_____

_____

_____

_____

_____

Discover your learning styles

I t's one thing to value learning and another to understand *how* you learn. Perhaps you've observed that people learn in different ways. Some like to think about facts and theories. Some learn by direct experience, while others learn by watching and reflecting. And some people are happiest when they feel a direct connection between their interests and their learning. There's a term that points to all these differences—*learning styles*. Our learning styles reveal much about who we are.

Understanding your learning styles offers direct benefits. With this knowledge, you can set up conditions to learn efficiently. You can absorb ideas quickly and learn a new task with less training. You can change jobs with more ease, multiply your career options, and find work that satisfies you.

What's more, knowing about learning styles allows you to work more effectively in teams. Knowing how people differ can help you understand your colleagues, give better instructions, delegate tasks, and resolve conflicts.

Learning takes place in modes

Psychologists create many theories about how people learn. One of the most widely used is David Kolb's theory of experiential learning.

According to Kolb, you learn constantly from your daily experiences. This learning occurs in four modes:

- *Concrete experience.* During this mode, you value ideas and procedures that have a personal meaning for you. A key phrase in this mode is *learning by feeling.*
- *Reflective observation.* Here you take time to plan and notice what's going on around you. In this mode, people learn by watching.
- *Abstract conceptualization.* Memorizing facts and mastering theories come into play in this mode, also described as learning by thinking.

- *Active experimentation.* During this mode, you apply ideas, test theories, and use new knowledge to influence others. This mode involves learning by doing.

To get a better idea of what takes place during these modes, reflect on your experience with career planning. You can begin by considering the benefits of career planning and making a personal connection to the topic (feeling). You can also visit a career-planning office and observe others using planning services (watching). Through reading and going to lectures, you discover many strategies for planning and job hunting (thinking). In addition, you can apply some of these strategies to see how well they work (doing).

Match activities to your learning style

Knowing your learning style preferences can be helpful when choosing your major and planning your career. You could focus on courses or jobs that suit your preferred modes of learning. Consulting with people who have different learning preferences can also be beneficial when you approach course work or other learning situations.

Styles combine modes

Most of us enjoy some stages of learning more than others, and this is how our learning styles develop. Kolb named four basic learning styles. Each style shows a preference for two modes:

- *Accommodators* combine feeling and doing. People with this style enjoy taking action. Accommodators often choose careers in management, sales, and promotion.
- *Divergers* combine feeling and watching. These people might opt for careers in the arts or social services.
- *Convergers* combine thinking and doing. This style is often valued in jobs where people review technical information to make decisions. Convergers often gravitate to careers in technology and applied sciences.

Resources on learning styles

The Learning Style Inventory is distributed by Hay/McBer, Inc., a human resources and management consulting company located at 116 Huntington Ave., Boston, MA 02116, 1-800-729-8074, trgmcber.haygroup.com.

Experiential Learning: Experience as the Source of Learning and Development by David A. Kolb (Englewood Cliffs, NJ: Prentice-Hall, 1984). This publication explains the theory of experiential learning—with applications to education, work, and personal development—and contains information on the validity of the Learning Style Inventory.

Adaptive Style Inventory by David A. Kolb and Richard Boyatzis, distributed by Hay/McBer, Boston, MA 02116. This inventory helps assess your adaptability in different learning situations.

Learning Skills Profile by David A. Kolb and Richard Boyatzis, distributed by Hay/McBer, Boston, MA 02116. This instrument compares your learning style to your job skill demands.

The 4MAT System: Teaching to Learning Style, with Right/Left Mode Techniques by Bernice McCarthy (Barrington, IL: About Learning, 1980, 1987). The 4MAT model explains learning in terms of the ways people perceive and process information.

Myers-Briggs Type Indicator and the Keirsey Temperament Sorter. The Keirsey Temperament Sorter, by David Keirsey, is a personality test that scores results according to the Myers-Briggs Type Indicator® instrument. The MBTI®, published by Consulting Psychologists Press, is a professional instrument that may be administered only by a certified examiner.

- *Assimilators* combine thinking and watching. People with this style enjoy research, mathematics, teaching, and writing.

Knowing that you have a strong preference for a certain learning style can help you choose a career. Working in any field tends to reinforce certain beliefs and behaviors. Discovering your learning style can help you find a career that's in tune with your values and preferences.

Ask for what you want

In school and in your career you might find that the way your instructor, co-worker or boss provides information is not always in the way you prefer learning or communicating. Once you have identified your preference, you can be more responsible for ensuring that your needs are met.

For example, according to Kolb, Mode 1 prefers to spend time observing others and planning before taking action. You probably enjoy working with others, too. Forming study groups or working in teams would be preferable.

If you have a strong preference for Mode 2, you are skilled in understanding theories and concepts. Chances are that you also enjoy solitary time and are not fond of working in groups.

If you have a strong preference for Mode 3, you probably excel at working with your hands and at laboratory stations. When in a learning situation, you are interested in knowing how things work. In addition you probably enjoy working alone or with a small group.

If you have a strong preference for Mode 4, you are skilled at teaching others what you have learned and helping them see the importance of these concepts. Whether in a learning situation or in everyday life, you like to apply facts and theories. You probably enjoy carrying out plans and having new and challenging experiences.

Expand your styles

According to Kolb, learning calls on us to resolve conflicts—the conflict between reflection and action, between concrete experience and abstract thinking. A skilled learner can move through all four stages of learning and keep them in creative tension.

Note that your learning styles can evolve and change over time. To develop a new style, work on project teams with people who learn differently than you. Also experiment. Look for situations in which you can safely practice new skills. If you enjoy learning by reading, for example, look for ways to apply new concepts or teach others what you know.

There are many online resources on learning styles. Visit the Houghton Mifflin Career Planning web site and access **Online Resources on Learning Styles** at **http://collegesurvival.college.hmco.com/students.** Consider exploring one or more of these assessments. Think about how your preferences can help lead you towards success in college and your career.

Discover the clues in your daily schedule

The way you spend time says a lot about your interests and values. Keeping a time log can be more than a time-management exercise. It can also reveal your passions, skills, interests—and a fruitful direction for your career.

To explore this idea, keep a time log for one week. On a separate sheet of paper, note what you did during each hour of each day. When the week is over, analyze the log. Instead of focusing on how well you used your time, look for the types of activity and the amount of time spent on each. How involved or joyful did you feel during each activity?

Pay special attention to your use of nonwork time. What did you do on weekends and holidays and at other times when there were no planning commitments? How did you choose to spend this time? Do these activities reveal an interest or preference to include in your career plan? Sum up your key observations here.

_____
_____
_____
_____
_____
_____
_____
_____
_____
_____
_____
_____
_____
_____

Discovery Statement

Write a list of your role models—the people you most admire. They may be people you know personally or people you have read or heard about. They may be alive or dead. They may be famous historical figures or not. Think of the people who have influenced your views and values positively.

_____
_____
_____
_____
_____
_____
_____
_____
_____
_____
_____
_____
_____
_____
_____
_____
_____
_____

Now, reflect on several questions. How have these people influenced you? What specifically do you admire in them? Does the fact that you've included these people on your list reveal anything about your preference for a career? Do these people have any personal qualities that impressed you? Have they pursued any vocations or projects that interest you? What career options or preferred ways of being do your answers suggest?

I learned that I …

_____
_____
_____
_____
_____
_____
_____

EXERCISE

Use a course to help set your course

One way to soak up career-planning ideas from your environment is by exploring a course catalog. By considering a new subject, you can open yourself to new career possibilities.

Skim through the catalog, quickly looking over every page. Note introductory classes in all the broad categories, such as fine arts, humanities, business, economics, and science and technology. After doing this, go back and focus on a subject or course that you normally consider "outside" your scope. Does the course sound interesting to you? Does it suggest a new career to explore? What training do people in this field complete? Write your reflections below.

_____

_____

_____

_____

_____

_____

_____

_____

_____

_____

_____

_____

EXERCISE

Assess your current skills

Before reading further, take 10 minutes to list all your work-related skills. Don't worry about following any special format. Just brainstorm as many of your skills as possible. One way to start is to focus on words ending in *ing*, such as *planning*, *reading*, or *creating*.

_____

_____

_____

_____

_____

_____

_____

_____

_____

Discover what you can _do_

The word _job_ brings to mind many other terms. Among them are _tasks, roles, duties, chores, responsibilities,_ and _functions._ One word comes closest to the heart of what we do in our careers. That word is _skill._

Skills are the anatomy, the "skeleton," of any job. They're at the core of what you offer an employer or customer. That means you can get a picture of any job you'd like to do by asking which skills it requires.

You develop skills constantly

One dictionary defines _skill_ as "the ability coming from one's knowledge, practice, aptitude, etc., to do something well." Skills are learned not only by taking advanced degrees or being in the work force for 20 years. Rather, any activity you improve with practice can be called a skill.

Just by going to school, relating to people, and pursuing your interests, you're constantly developing skills. If you can run a meeting, organize your study area, plant a garden, comfort a troubled friend, or draw interesting doodles, you've got skills that are worth money.

Multiply your skills by magic

With practice, people can expand their list of skills from zero to several hundred. Such an empowering discovery can just as well be yours. The secret is knowing ways to spot a skill so that it leaps out of the pages of your life story.

Keep in mind that there are at least two kinds of skills: content skills and transferable skills. By taking into account both skill groups, many people find their career possibilities expanding instantly.

Content skills reflect how much a person knows about a certain subject or how well she can handle a specific procedure. Someone who can speak Spanish like a native or repair a car transmission has content skills. So does a person who can program a computer, fix a broken TV, or play the piano in a professional jazz group. In each case, she's using a specialized knowledge or ability.

Transferable skills are general abilities that can apply to many different subjects. For example, if you do well at writing term papers in history, you will probably write well about computers, English literature, or anything else. In each case, you're comparing, analyzing, and combining ideas—using the same transferable skills. By recognizing transferable skills, you can expand your career options.

Following are more examples of transferable skills:

Attending to detail
Budgeting
Calculating
Caring for people
Coaching
Consulting
Counseling
Designing
Diagnosing problems
Drawing
Editing
Estimating costs
Evaluating ideas
Following instructions
Gathering facts
Inspecting
Interpreting data
Keeping records
Leading meetings
Learning
Listening
Managing money
Managing projects
Memorizing
Negotiating
Observing
Operating machines
Organizing
Performing in the arts
Persuading
Planning
Playing games
Reading
Scheduling
Selling
Solving problems
Speaking
Supervising
Taking inventory
Taking notes
Taking risks
Teaching
Using a computer
Using mechanical tools

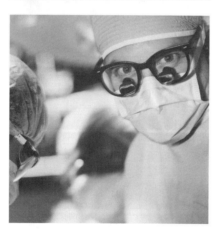

This is only a partial list. You can learn to recognize many more.

When you fill out a job application, write a résumé, or go on a job interview, you're talking the language of skills. Recognizing all your skills can inspire confidence and help you communicate the full range of your abilities.

EXERCISE

Recognize skills

This exercise in recognizing skills includes three steps. It will take about one hour to complete.

Step 1

On 3×5 cards, list your common activities. To refresh your memory, review what you've done in the past week or month. Recall as many activities as you can and list each one on a separate card. Some of your cards might read "washed dishes," "tuned up my car," or "tutored a French class." Do this for 20 minutes.

Step 2

Next, look over your activity cards. Then take another 20 minutes to list any specialized knowledge or procedures needed to complete these activities. These are your content skills. For example, tutoring a French class requires the ability to speak French. Tuning a car requires knowing how to adjust a car's timing and replace spark plugs. You may list several content skills for any one activity. Write each skill on a separate card and label it "Content."

Step 3

Go over your activity cards one more time. Do you see any examples of transferable skills? As you do this step, refer to the list of transferable skills in "Discover what you can *do*." For example, giving a speech and working as a salesperson in a stereo store both require persuading people. Tutoring in French requires explaining, listening well, and speaking clearly. Tuning a car means you probably can attend to details and trouble-shoot. Write each skill on a separate card and label it "transferable."

By doing this exercise, you draw a detailed picture of your skills. Keep your lists of content skills and transferable skills to use in writing your résumé, preparing for interviews, and other career-planning tasks. As you think of new skills, ad to these lists.

JOURNAL ENTRY

Discovery Statement

Take the lists of content skills and transferable skills you just created. Compare them with the skills you listed in the exercise "Assess your current skills" on page 32. Has your picture of your career skills changed after doing the previous exercises? How?

I discovered that I ...

_____

_____

_____

_____

_____

EXERCISE

Link your skills to achievements

All of us have completed a difficult or challenging task that required our best efforts. For some of these achievements, we receive rewards or lasting praise. Others get only fleeting recognition. Remembering both kinds of achievements can help us become more aware of our skills.

For this exercise, list as many achievements as you can recall. Identify the skills you used in accomplishing each one. For example:

Achievement	Skill Used
Hired for part-time job	Speaking
	Writing
	Persuading people
Coached a baseball team	Supervising people
	Speaking
	Teaching

Include any activity you found personally rewarding, whether or not it received formal recognition. Make your list on a separate sheet of paper.

When you've finished, circle the three achievements that give you the greatest sense of satisfaction. Do these point to any skills you'd like to use in your career? List those skills below.

_____

_____

_____

_____

Explore vocational assessments

Vocational assessments are another resource for self-discovery and are helpful tools in career planning. These assessments might also be called *vocational aptitude tests, skill inventories,* or *interest assessments.* They provide useful information about personality, comfort with technology, and work preferences. Your school's career-planning, counseling, or job placement center may offer one of more of these assessments. Be sure to inquire as part of your career planning. Ask if there is a cost and if anyone will review the results with you.

The following are some better-known vocational assessments. Bear in mind that they are not tests. There are no right or wrong answers to the questions they ask. Also remember that they won't choose your career for you. Each is a source of information.

California Psychological Inventory   The California Psychological Inventory provides a view of your professional and personal style by measuring a range of individual differences: interpersonal skills, social skills, values, achievement-seeking needs, and stylistic modes. The inventory also measures managerial potential and creative temperament.

Career Ability Placement Survey (CAPS)
CAPS provides you with information about your abilities. It helps you understand your potential, your strengths, and your weaknesses, and it gives you a prediction of success in various types of occupations.

Career Thoughts Inventory   This vocational assessment can help you uncover negative thoughts that may impede effective, successful career planning. The inventory provides suggestions about how to change negative thoughts to positive ones required for good career choices.

Eureka Skills Inventory   This inventory is a card-sorting skills assessment that includes the skills you normally use at work or for daily activities. You sort the skills you enjoy using into categories: very satisfying, moderately satisfying, or somewhat satisfying. Your choices are mapped by a computer to show the ways you would prefer to spend your time on the job and the types of occupations that use the skills you have selected in the assessment.

Hall Occupational Orientation Inventory (HOOI)
This values inventory is designed to help you rank personal factors that are important aspects of choosing your career. The HOOI gives you information about your interests, abilities, needs, and values.

Myers-Briggs Type Indicator® (MBTI) Instrument
The MBTI provides insight about yourself and how someone like you fits into the world of work, working with others of similar and different profiles. Results provide personal awareness and help you identify careers and work environments where you are most likely to thrive and feel fulfilled.

Personal Career Development Profile (PCDP)
The PCDP shows you how your personality relates to your career plans and potential job performance. The Profile provides you with insights into your choices and preferences, emphasizing your personal strengths, including an analysis of your approach to problem solving and stress management.

Self-Directed Search (SDS)   The SDS asks you to answer a questionnaire about your interests and abilities. Upon completion, you receive a computerized report that provides you with a personality summary code. The report then lists occupations and fields of study that correlate with your personality code. You can begin career exploration with a list of occupations at your fingertips.

Strong Interest Inventory   This inventory helps you identify your interests and matches them with possible occupations. It measures interests rather than abilities and compares your likes and dislikes to those of people who are satisfied in specific careers.

Vocational Preference Inventory (VPI)   This inventory is a brief personality test based on the theory that occupations can be based on personality traits. It is especially useful to people who have had ambiguous results on other vocational assessments.

 For more resources on vocational assessments, including links to web sites featuring the assessments mentioned in this article, visit Houghton Mifflin's Career Planning web site: **http://collegesurvival.college.hmco.com/students.**

Job skills for the new millennium

In the early 1990s, the U.S. Department of Labor began issuing reports created by the Secretary's Commission on Achieving Necessary Skills (SCANS). This series of documents—called the *SCANS reports*—lists skills to promote success for workers as they enter this new century. You can use these influential documents to develop your résumé, plan your career, and link your school experiences to the world of work. The SCANS reports identify three foundations (basic skills, thinking skills, and personal qualities) and five core competencies (resources, interpersonal skills, information, systems, and technology). More details about each of these follow.

As a student, you are already developing many of the skills listed in the SCANS reports. Remember that employers might hire you for demonstrated evidence of these skills—even more than for years of experience in your chosen field.

Three foundations

Basic skills

- Reading to locate, understand, and interpret written information
- Writing to communicate ideas and information
- Using arithmetic to perform basic computations and solve problems
- Listening to interpret and respond to verbal messages and other cues

Thinking skills

- Speaking to inform and persuade others
- Creative thinking to generate new ideas
- Decision making to set and meet goals
- Problem solving to identify challenges and implement action plans
- Seeing things in the mind's eye to interpret and create symbols, pictures, graphs, and other visual tools
- Knowing how to learn

Personal qualities

- Responsibility to exert high effort and persist in meeting goals
- Self-esteem to maintain a positive view of your abilities
- Social skills that demonstrate adaptability and empathy
- Self-management to assess yourself accurately, set personal goals, and monitor personal progress

Five core competencies

Resources

- Allocating time for goal-relevant activities
- Allocating money to prepare budgets and meet them
- Allocating materials and facilities
- Allocating human resources to assign tasks effectively and provide others with feedback

Interpersonal skills

- Participating as a member of a team
- Teaching others
- Serving clients and customers
- Exercising leadership
- Negotiating to reach agreements
- Working with diversity

Information

- Acquiring and evaluating information
- Organizing and maintaining information
- Interpreting and communicating information in oral, written, and visual forms
- Using computers to process information

Systems

- Understanding how social and technological systems operate
- Monitoring and correcting performance
- Improving or designing systems

Technology

- Selecting appropriate technology
- Applying technology to tasks
- Maintaining and troubleshooting technology

 Adapted from U.S. Department of Labor, *Skills and Tasks for Jobs: A SCANS Report for America 2000.* 1992. Access it online at wdr.doleta.gov/SCANS/whatwork/whatwork.html.

EXERCISE

Expand your skills

List skills you think will be valued in the workplace 20 years from now. (Review the previous article for ideas.) Then write one action you will take to increase your proficiency at each skill you listed. Set a due date for taking each action.

Come back to this exercise periodically to update your plan and develop new skills.

Skill	Action	Due date

Discover what you _have_

B egin career planning with full knowledge of your assets. Assets are things you have that you can use to your advantage in the job market. Discovering your assets is a powerful way to round out what you've already discovered about your values (who you are) and your skills (what you can do).

Another way to think of assets is as resources. You can draw on these resources in your next job search or career change.

Explore your assets in depth by doing the next exercise.

EXERCISE

List your assets

Other exercises in this chapter encourage you to explore your personal qualities and unique skills. Now, take a few minutes to consider and write about the remaining resources that you bring to career planning. Considering these factors now can help you as you complete job applications, write résumés, and do other career-planning tasks.

Continue your responses on separate paper if needed.

Financial resources

Think about ways to finance your next career change or job hunt. Will you look for a new job while working full-time or part-time? Can you take time to design your next career step without feeling financial pressure? Do you have savings, investments, or other equity you can draw on while you look for a job? Briefly describe your financial assets.

_____

_____

_____

_____

_____

Contacts

Now consider the people in your life who can assist you in meeting your career goals. These can include friends, relatives, coworkers (present and past), members of professional organizations to which you belong, and anyone else who comes to mind. List the names of those people.

_____

_____

_____

_____

_____

(Continued on p. 40)

Recognized learning

Describe the formal recognition you've received for your prior learning. List any educational degrees that you've earned. Also include continuing education hours, majors, minors, and any courses you've taken for credit, even if they don't relate to any formal degree. If your prior work experience gives you a favorable reputation in your field, include this fact in your description also.

_____

_____

_____

_____

_____

_____

_____

_____

_____

_____

_____

Experience

Briefly describe any experiences that relate to your chosen career or field. List all the jobs you've held, including part-time and summer employment. Also list volunteer work, internships, and any household duties that developed career-related skills.

_____

_____

_____

_____

_____

_____

_____

_____

_____

_____

_____

Other

Take a minute to review what you've written so far. Now add to your list, including any other assets that can move you toward the careers of your choice.

_____

_____

_____

_____

_____

_____

_____

_____

_____

_____

_____

_____

_____

_____

_____

_____

_____

_____

_____

_____

_____

_____

_____

_____

_____

_____

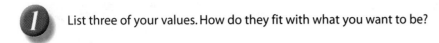

1. List three of your values. How do they fit with what you want to be?

2. Why is it important to know about your learning style and the learning styles of others?

3. What are some of your skills that you think will be transferable to the career you are planning?

4. In which of the five core competencies are you strongest? Explain your answer.

5. How will your assets help you as you complete job applications, write résumés, and do other career-planning tasks?

CHAPTER 3

Discover Work

I never see what has to be done. I only see what remains to be done.
MARIE CURIE

The best that an individual can do is to concentrate on what he or she can do, in the course of a burning effort to do it better.
ELIZABETH BOWEN

IN THIS CHAPTER . . . You've got a world of choices. Use multiple resources to learn more about the world of work—and then jump right in. Gain related experience through information interviews, internships, and the Internet. Connect to cyberspace and use online resources to plan your career.

You've got a world of choices

Our society offers a limitless array of careers. You no longer need to limit yourself to a handful of traditional categories, such as business, education, government, or manufacturing. The number of job titles is expanding so rapidly that we can barely track them.

In addition, people are constantly creating new services to meet emerging needs. Today some people work as ritual consultants, helping to plan weddings, anniversaries, graduations, and other ceremonies. Space planners specialize in helping businesses and individuals arrange furniture and equipment efficiently. Auto brokers will do research, shop around, and buy a car for you.

Freelance organizers will walk into your home or office and advise you on managing paperwork. Pet psychologists will help train your dog to stop barking at the neighbors. And life coaches will offer you partnership in creating a wonderful life.

Almost any experience can lead to insights that help us choose a career. This includes anything from watching television commercials or petting a dog to eating fast food or flipping through a magazine.

All the goods and services in our society result from work done by people. Thinking about this may give you new leads for career planning. In the midst of any activity, wherever you are, you can ask: How did the work of other human beings help create the experience I'm having now? Each day we encounter dozens of working people. They're supervising, building, teaching, learning, consulting, writing, speaking, cleaning, organizing, and much more. They're producing cards, books, furniture, computers, houses, offices, schools, food, and more—everything created by human beings. By consciously investigating this fact, we can open up an abundant range of options for a career.

As you read and use this chapter, you can start gathering information on available careers. You can also find out how to organize and act on that information. Clearly there is no reason to limit your choices too soon.

You've got the universe to choose from.

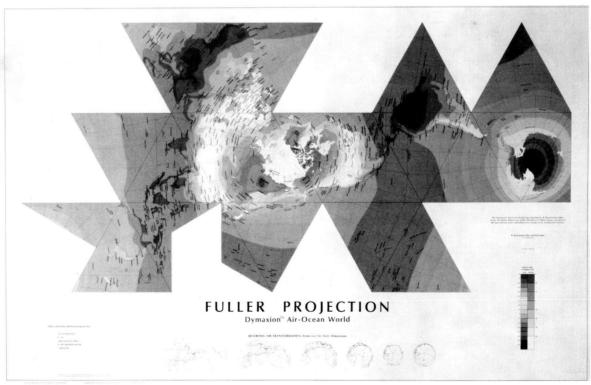

FULLER PROJECTION
Dymaxion™ Air-Ocean World

EXERCISE

Dig out the "life story" of a product or service

Pick any object near the place where you study. If possible, choose something that holds a special interest for you. Examples are books, records, tapes, pens, pencils, computers, or clothing. Or if you wish, think of one service you know about. This could be anything from dry cleaning or television repair to counseling or insurance sales.

Then ask yourself how the product or service you chose was created. Describe its purpose or the need it fills. Are there other ways to satisfy this need? Trace the history of this product or service, listing the steps required to create it. If you can't list all these steps, do some research to find out more about them. List your ideas on 3×5 cards.

Next, ask what people performed each of the steps in creating this product or service. What were their job titles? What tasks make up their work? What training do they have? Are you interested in learning more about their careers? List those careers on cards also.

EXERCISE

Use a magazine to plan your career

Spend 15 minutes glancing through a magazine or newspaper. Notice the articles, people in photographs, and illustrations. As you do, keep several questions in mind. What are the people described as or depicted doing? What goods or services are being provided? What careers are described or shown? Watch TV or listen to the radio for one hour, asking the same questions about the people you see and hear. Did you get any ideas for a career you'd like to find out more about? List your ideas here:

_____
_____
_____
_____
_____
_____
_____
_____
_____
_____
_____
_____
_____
_____
_____
_____
_____
_____
_____
_____

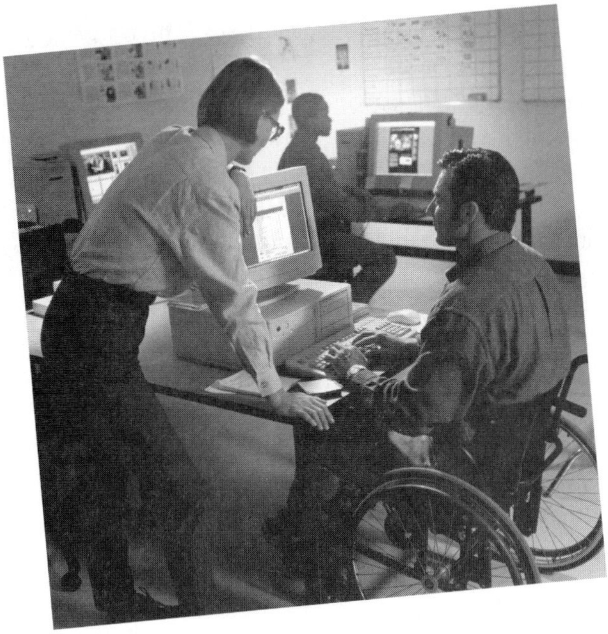

Learn more about the world of work

To find out about the universe of jobs out there, you can turn to many sources. These include family members, books, tapes, friends, counselors, teachers, religious leaders, and people who work in your field of interest.

Sources of career and job information vary greatly from place to place. By starting with the following list, you can quickly locate more resources in your area:

- Bookstores and public or school libraries. It's possible to find materials on career planning in almost any library. In addition, libraries may subscribe to professional journals in career areas of interest to you. Ask your librarian about videotapes, audiotapes, newsletters, Internet sites, and films on career planning.

- Counseling centers, career-planning agencies, and job placement centers at your school

- The U.S. Department of Human Resources, Employment Office

- Local welfare-to-work programs

- Career-planning courses offered by schools, community education programs, churches, the YMCA or YWCA, and other service organizations or community groups

- State employment offices

- Private career-planning firms

- Private employment agencies and career counselors

- Local businesses

- Your local Chamber of Commerce

- Professional organizations and associations

- Trade unions

- The U.S. Armed Forces

- TV specials on employment trends, the economy, and career planning. Also look for specials on people whose careers interest you.

- Your congressional representative or senator, state representative or senator, and city council or school board members

Two government publications have become standard references for career planners. One is the *Dictionary of Occupational Titles,* a kind of encyclopedia that describes and classifies hundreds of jobs. *The Occupational Outlook Handbook* lists the prospects for employment in many of those jobs. It also provides details on entry requirements, salaries, and working conditions. Both can be useful places to start your research into the work world.

The tremendous growth in the number of computers coupled with easy access to the Internet and the near universal availability of printers has made a huge array of career information instantly available at little or no cost. Richard Bolles, author of *What Color Is Your Parachute?* has an excellent web site at **http://www.JobHuntersBible. com**. He organizes career information around five ways the Internet can be used in career planning:

1 To find job listings

2 To help with résumés and cover letters

3 To obtain career counseling

4 To search for career-related research

5 To make contacts with others

The Internet can help in other more specific ways too, such as career assessment and online job application. Assessment users beware. Although assessment services are free at some sites, most charge an access fee.

Overwhelmed by all the options? Computer resources are relatively easy to use, requiring only that you click your mouse a few times to get the information you want. Spend

an hour or so surfing the Web to locate information that is important to you.

Visiting any of the sites listed below will help get you started. Your librarian or school's career center can help you find more.

Career Resource Center at **http://www.careers.org** is a great source of career-related material as well as job-hunting links.

America's Job Bank at **http://www.ajb.dni.us** features labor market information as well as a nationwide job database.

FedWorld at **http://www.fedworld.gov/jobs/jobsearch.html** is the official site for U.S. government job openings.

National Urban League at **http://www.nul.org/career** offers Job Bank information in cooperation with Monster.com.

JOURNAL ENTRY

Intention Statement

Knowing about sources of career information and using them are two different experiences. Shift into the action mode by committing to use three career-planning resources in the next week. Complete the following statement:

I intend to use the following career-planning resources in the next seven days:

1. _____

2. _____

3. _____

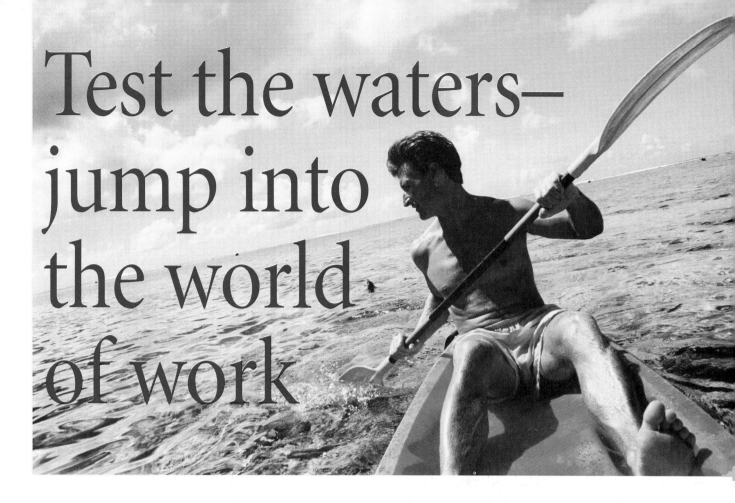

Test the waters— jump into the world of work

Information you gather from a library, the Internet, a book, or a counselor can add a lot of specifics to your career plan. You can also immerse yourself in the work world and gain knowledge directly.

Students commonly report the value of observing and interviewing people at work. This kind of research can open your eyes to career options, help you test your choices, and let you connect with other people. Jumping right into the work world can raise your energy level and commitment to career planning. Following are several ways to mine this rich resource.

Do information interviews

As you research careers, talk to local employers and people who actually do the job you'd like to do. Schedule an information interview to ask them about their work. Make it clear that your purpose is not to apply for work but to research your career. With their permission, go to their job sites. Spend time with them during a workday. Hang around. Ask questions.

Talking to potential employers now, while you're in school, promotes some of the most powerful learning about careers. Information interviews offer a chance to warm up for job interviews. They also close the gap between your perceptions and the realities of the workplace.

To get the most out of your information interview, first research the field you've chosen and the particular business or organization you're going to visit. When you arrive for the interview, respect the person's schedule and the demands of her job. Also, don't use an information interview to ask for a job. Employers often feel betrayed by people who use this tactic.

There is no need to be shy about contacting people for information interviews. Chances are they will be flattered by your request. If someone turns you down for an interview, politely ask if she can recommend someone else.

Before your interview, prepare a list of questions, such as these:

- How did you enter this line of work?
- What do you do on a typical day?
- What kinds of problems and decisions do you regularly face?
- What do you like most and least about your job?
- How can I prepare for this line of work?
- What changes are occurring in this field?
- What are the opportunities for promotions?

- How do people learn about jobs in this field?
- Do you have any special advice for a new person entering this field?
- Is there a salary range for this job?
- Can you suggest other people I can talk with about this career?

The people you interview can provide insights available nowhere else. One of the best sources of career information is yours for the asking.

Work with others

Another way to research the work world is to join with others. Pair up with a friend to do career research. Or form a career-planning study group. Each member can gather information or interview people in fields of mutual interest, then report back to the group. You can also team up to go to information interviews.

Working in groups allows you to give one another feedback on goals and plans. You can brainstorm about resources and tools for reaching those goals and you can even help one another look for jobs.

A group can help you sharpen your thinking. Other people might spot a flaw or gap in your career plan. Asking for their suggestions is a powerful way to do a "reality check."

At the same time, taking part in a group can open you up to your dreams. Others may point out facts or sources of information you've overlooked. They may point out career choices you've never considered or skills you were not aware you had.

Volunteer

Volunteering at a place where you'd like to work is an effective method for job research. To get the most out of volunteer experience, find a job that matches your skills. Research and choose volunteer positions as carefully as you would a full-time salaried job.

To begin, identify organizations that are doing work that interests you. Starting with your local office of the United Way or the Red Cross, find the names of human services organizations. Also consider for-profit businesses providing goods or services you value. Then identify specific people in each organization to contact, and ask each for an information interview.

Work

To find out more about working, work. Beyond gaining work experience, you can learn about careers firsthand. A job can also help you choose skills to develop further. All this feedback can sharpen and refine your career plan.

Consider an internship or a cooperative education program. Internships are formal ways to gain work experience while attending school. They provide work opportunities that blend classroom learning with employment in a specific field. Internships vary, ranging from paid jobs to volunteer work. Some award academic credit, and others do not. Some are for only a month or less, others for as long as a year. Internships are often designed so that an onsite supervisor teaches, directs, or explains the job to participating students.

Cooperative education programs offer another kind of work experience. This special type of internship is more

Getting Involved

If you are looking for additional ways to become involved in your community—whether it be on your college campus or in your local town—the opportunities are plentiful but may need some seeking out.

Start by networking, just like you would if you were looking for a job. Ask friends and family members if they know of local organizations looking for volunteers. Consider conferring with your local place of worship. Review your college's web site to see if any groups on campus are planning events. Search the Internet. In order to identify an organization that does work that interests you and supports your values and beliefs, review their web site. Read their mission statement. Send an email your area coordinator and volunteer at an upcoming event.

To get started in your search, visit these web sites:
Habitat for Humanity (**http://www.habitat.org/**)
The Boys and Girls Club of America (**http://www.bgca.org**)
Big Brother, Big Sister (**http://www.bbbsa.org/**)
The American Red Cross (**http://www.redcross.org/**)
United Way (**http://national.unitedway.org/**)

formalized. It combines classroom study with supervised, practical experience in a given field.

Turn a "lousy" job into a loving teacher

Every job can teach you something about the world of work and yourself.

To learn the most effective lessons from a job you do not enjoy, practice taking another view of it. Imagine that your main purpose at this job is research. This grounds your work in learning. Ask some questions: What can I teach myself from this work experience? Can I turn my insights into strategies for finding a more enjoyable career? Am I learning any skills at this job that I can transfer to my chosen career? You can answer these questions at the same time you're making plans to find a new job.

Say you're employed in an entry-level job in a fast-food restaurant. You dislike the job, but you need the money. To turbo-charge this experience, observe what's going on. Ask questions. Find out why things are done in a certain way. Volunteer to do new jobs. Show a genuine interest in the business. Look at everyone's job tasks, noting the way the product moves from preparation to the customer. Make suggestions that improve the service or work flow. With a little creative thinking, you can use any job for your own purpose.

JOURNAL ENTRY

Intention Statement

Choose one of the techniques listed in "Test the waters—jump into the world of work." Then follow up on that technique. List the technique here, along with two or three types of action you can take to use it. Also list a deadline for taking such action.

I intend to . . .

_____

_____

_____

_____

_____

_____

_____

Gaining related experience– being an intern

One way to start your career path off on the right foot is by gaining real career experience through internships. Once you've narrowed down the career options you have considered, an internship can provide you with hands-on research to find out about the daily workings of someone in your career field. Begin by inquiring about internship programs at a prospective employer. You will likely have to submit a résumé and cover letter explaining your interest. Even companies that do not have formal internship programs may accept applications. Keep in mind that many interns do not get paid; consider speaking with your academic advisor about gaining class credit.

As an intern you can gain invaluable skills. You will likely be asked to perform administrative duties that will allow you to obtain experience with professional phone etiquette and written business correspondence, and you will be given the opportunity to work with other people in positions you may be interested in pursuing. Internships are great places to learn about organizational culture and to build relationships for networking.

After you have completed your internship, review your experience. If the company and positions available were aligned with your career goals, your role as an intern may help lead to permanent job offers following graduation. Keep in close touch with the contacts you make—they may be working at another company when you graduate and can help get your foot in the door. Even if you find that the company, atmosphere, or tasks did not meet your expectations, you will have gained valuable skills that will make you more employable at a future position. You also will be able to create a list of criteria that you want your next job to include. Be sure to incorporate the skills and experiences from your internship on your résumé— no matter what job you choose.

JOURNAL ENTRY

Intention Statement

Complete the following sentences.

I will find the names, addresses, and phone numbers of several people working in the following careers:

_____
_____
_____
_____
_____

I will write or call these people on the following dates to schedule information interviews:

_____
_____
_____
_____
_____

JOURNAL ENTRY

Discovery Statement

List any jobs you've had that you didn't like. Then ask yourself if you learned anything from them that can help you plan your career.

I discovered that I . . .

_____
_____
_____
_____
_____
_____
_____
_____
_____
_____
_____

Imagine a world without jobs

We are on the edge of a radical shift in the nature of work—a change so profound that few can predict its course. This change could be as dislocating and far-reaching as the Industrial Revolution, when millions of people moved off farms and began working in factories, changing their lives forever.

International competition, corporate downsizing, and new technology are making the job as we know it a thing of the past. People will still do lots of work throughout the twenty-first century. That work could be structured around temporary projects and flexible teams instead of lifelong employment. Constant career planning is already becoming a condition of survival.

Security vanishes

During the 1950s, many North Americans enjoyed boom times. Millions of people joined the middle class. The "American dream" centered on material security—getting a job that lasted until retirement, buying a house, and driving a new car every two years.

After 1980, the American dream suffered. Corporations tightened their belts. Workers with decades of experience were laid off. Middle-aged, mid-level executives found themselves out on the street. Though computer technology created jobs, it eroded employment in some fields. The number of "good jobs" appeared to shrink. Although the U.S. Department of Labor reported that over 16 million new jobs were created in the 1990s, less than half paid over $7 an hour. In 1998, as a result of the increase in the number of low-paying jobs, over half of American families required two or more incomes to maintain their living standard.

In this new economy, no job is truly secure. Any of us at any time could join the ranks of career changers and job hunters.

Changing conditions, changing work

To gain perspective, remember that relatively speaking, jobs were created only yesterday. Before the eighteenth century, no one had "jobs." People farmed or worked independently at crafts. There was no need for career planning. No one had a "career."

During the late 1700s and early 1800s, this changed. Factory owners hired people to work long hours at central locations away from home. "Jobs" came into being.

Most of us take the concept of jobs for granted. Yet in the new economy of the past few years, the very conditions that created jobs—mass production, assembly lines, heavy industry—have undergone major changes. For example, in the manufacturing sector, which for decades has been the backbone of the U.S. economy, the number of jobs shrunk in each of the past 10 years. Entire segments have disappeared altogether. Typewriters are no longer made in the United States. In 2001, over 40 percent of new cars in the United States were imported. Today, not a single American automaker claims its cars are made entirely in the United States.

Millions of people now work with computers, not big machines. These people manipulate data, not things—a fact that can make jobs disappear. Data does not require factory supervisors, inventory managers, or many other people in traditional jobs.

Armed with new technology, many companies find that they can trim employees and still make a profit. With a laptop, printer, modem, and cellular phone, a sales rep can turn a car into an office on wheels—no secretary required.

In this emerging economy, many people make money without jobs. According to the U.S. Department of Labor, over half of all American workers in the year 2001 were temporary, part-time, or contract workers—many of them white-collar professionals. Today, the biggest "employer" in America is not IBM, GMC, the federal government, or even the high-tech Intel. It is Manpower, a temporary employment agency.

Much of this change is driven by sheer speed. Competition and technology increase the pace of work. Money flows to companies that produce faster, sell faster, and service faster. In this atmosphere, traditional jobs can slow response time and decrease flexibility.

To prosper, adjust your thinking

You can prosper in the new economy. Even if you never have a job, you can still do fulfilling work and make plenty of money. You could "telecommute" and work from a computer at home. You could freelance or work on contract. Even if you work for a company, you can think like a consultant and move freely between projects and teams.

Changed conditions call for changed thinking. Some of what people "know" about careers could dim your prospects. Think critically about statements such as these:

- "Just get a good job and you'll be set for life."

- "You can't do that—it's not in your job description."

- "Just coast for a few years until you retire."

In their place, consider these ideas:

- "Everyone is self-employed. Think like a vendor who's hired to complete a specific task. Demonstrate your value in each project and plan to change jobs often."

- Do what it takes to get the job done—even if it's not in your job description."

- "No one can afford to coast. Develop new skills and learn constantly."

Rapid change creates new needs. You can use your skills to meet those needs.

In the competitive job market of the twenty-first century, education, training, and skill development are more important than ever. These qualities increase your versatility in the new economy. Only low-paying, entry-level jobs require little or no training.

Further your education

Getting more education is a wise choice. It demonstrates a spirit of adventure and has a way of enriching our lives and getting our creative juices flowing. Not only will you become more knowledgeable, but you will be able to meet others and develop a supporting network. Remember to seek out opportunities. Welfare-to-work programs offer training in many entry-level jobs. Many colleges offer distance-learning options and have expanded the days and hours of on-campus instruction. Enrolling in a class is easier than ever before. Both the number and type of courses available on the Internet and educational TV have grown by leaps and bounds. Some of these courses are available 24 hours a day, seven days a week.

For most of us, it's now possible to enroll in a class any time it's convenient. The public library, nearby colleges, and public television stations can help you identify what's available in your local area.

Consider upgrading and adding computer skills

Computers are here to stay. Ten years ago it was okay if you didn't have computer skills. Since then, the range of jobs requiring some level of computer skills has increased dramatically. In today's job market, anyone who enters without any computer skills has seriously limited his or her employment options. Even if you're not sure of your career field, developing or upgrading computer skills is a smart investment; it's hard to identify a promising future that doesn't require some level of computer skills.

Training options have also expanded over the years. With computer technology advancing every 6 to 10 months, the number and type of computer courses have grown. Today, it is not unusual for colleges to offer 20 or more different computer-related courses, varying in length from a few hours to a semester or more. Use the educational resources suggested here to identify the training options available in your area. If you're not sure where to begin, consider developing keyboarding and basic word-processing skills as a start. Check the job listings in your local area for clues about the computer skills that are in demand.

Gain a financial cushion

In the new economy, people who live from paycheck to paycheck could feel like dinosaurs—their financial health might become extinct. To avoid this fate, manage money with a potential job loss in mind. Create your own ways to fund health care and retirement. Look for ways to increase your income and decrease your spending. Save money to cushion yourself through a career transition or job loss.

Learn to manage stress

Job hunting can isolate people, and unemployment can create stress. To thrive amid change, find ways to maintain your physical and mental health. Focus on the factors you can control and let go of the rest. Create zones of stability in your life—relationships and projects that outlast jobs. Through workshops, books, and other resources, learn to manage stress with skill.

Plan to get laid off

Think about what you'd do if you lost your job today. Create a career plan with several scenarios. Have a "plan B" for your career—and plans C, D, and E. Doing so increases your flexibility and expands your thinking, even if you never have to implement an alternate plan.

Detach

Many people identify with their jobs. They define themselves as accountants, technical writers, sales representatives, or stockbrokers. When their jobs go out the window, so does their identity.

For maximum flexibility, detach. Remember that you are not your job or your current career. Shift your identity to your core values and fundamental commitments. When your jobs change, your values can remain. Think of work as a series of new opportunities to live out your life purpose and contribute to others.

EXERCISE

Create a career

Compile a list of careers that have been created only in the past decade—or that could be created in the next decade. Some possible examples: computer security officers, health care cost specialists, recycling consultants, and robotic engineers. Write your ideas on 3×5 cards.

As you make this list, think about any problems in our society that call for new solutions. See if you can invent new careers to promote those solutions. Finally, look for ideas to add to your own career plan.

Connect to cyberspace

The Internet is a complex of computer networks used by people across the world. Connecting to this network gives you access to millions of pages of text, animation, audio clips, video clips, and more. Through this connection you can expand your experience of diversity with a few clicks on a computer mouse. You can link to people across the world and explore a vast array of cultures and countries. They're just about all present in cyberspace.

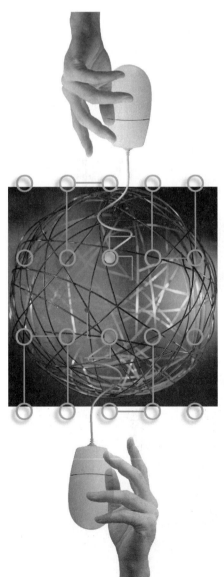

Choosing hardware and software

To enter this multimedia world, you'll need some computer hardware (equipment) and software (programs that allow you to use the equipment). Equipment usually includes a keyboard, a CPU (central processing unit), a monitor (the "screen"), a printer, and a modem (a device that sends data over telephone or cable lines). Laptop computers combine the keyboard, CPU, and monitor into one portable unit.

You might also use a scanner (which transfers text and images from paper to a computer disk) and a CD drive that allows you to access data on compact discs and write (save) date on them.

When shopping for a computer, remember the "five S's": storage, software, speed, sight, and savings.

Storage. Personal computers store data in two ways. One is random access memory (RAM) or primary storage, which is the amount of data the computer can instantly manage without accessing its secondary storage. Secondary storage is the hard disk, which stores data permanently.

When it comes to storage, more is usually better. Having more RAM will help you fly faster on the Internet. And having a lot of hard disk space will allow you to store more software

and more of the documents that you create or download from the Internet.

Software. Next, think about the basic software for your computer—its operating system. The operating system is also called a *platform*.

In personal computers, the most popular platforms are Windows and Macintosh. (Computers with the Windows platform are called *PCs*.) These two platforms are different, and transferring data between them can be tricky. A reasonable option is to choose the platform most likely to be used by people in your major.

Word processing software handles many writing and other basic tasks. And you'll need specific software to browse the Internet. Netscape Communicator and Microsoft Internet Explorer are two widely used browsers.

Speed. A computer's speed is determined by the kind of chip that powers its processor. Go for the fastest chip you can afford. Chip speed is often rated in megahertz. The higher the megahertz, the faster the computer.

You'll use a telephone or cable modem to connect to the Internet. Again, get the fastest connection you can afford. This will save you time when you access the Internet.

Sight. If you have any dollars left, channel them into getting the best monitor you can afford. Look for a monitor that delivers high resolution images in millions of colors, and go for a monitor that will be easy on your eyes. If you find yourself spending hours at the computer to finish a paper or create a presentation, you'll be thankful you spent money on a quality monitor.

Savings. Overall, personal computer prices are falling, even as these computers offer more speed, storage, and other goodies. But read ads carefully: Package prices might not include everything you need. Scout out student discounts. Find out if your school gives grants or loans to fund computer purchases.

Also determine whether your computer purchase is tax-deductible. It might be if you're attending school to maintain your current job.

Remember that there are plenty of alternatives to buying a new computer. One is to buy used equipment that you can upgrade if you choose. Another is to scout out computers that you can use for free or at low cost. Check for a student computer lab on your campus or at a public library.

Accessing the Internet

Currently there are several ways for you to access the Internet. One option is an Internet service provider (ISP) that offers basic Internet access to individuals for a flat monthly fee. Look for them in your local phone directory.

Commercial online services such as America Online offer another option. Such services offer Internet access plus additional online features of their own.

Before signing up for any service, ask whether you pay a flat monthly fee or a per-hour fee for connecting to the Internet.

Discovering what's there

The World Wide Web. The area of the Internet that gets the most publicity is the World Wide Web, which is growing exponentially by millions of pages. Information on the Web is organized and displayed as colorful sites, some with many "pages." You can move through pages in any sequence by clicking on highlighted or underlined words called *hyperlinks*. Never mind that the computer that originates the page might be thousands of miles away. Those pages show up on your screen in a matter of seconds or minutes, depending on the type of Internet connection you have.

Email (electronic mail). With a computer and modem, you can send email to anyone who's also connected to the Internet. Using email, you can send your message down the information highway almost instantly—no stamp or trip to the post office necessary. People in almost every country in the world can now receive email. Check to see if your school offers free email accounts for students.

Chat rooms. Chat rooms connect you with other people who share your interests. These services allow people to carry on instantaneous conversations in "real" time by typing messages to each other from their computers. Chat rooms exist on almost any subject.

Usenet (newsgroups). Computerized bulletin boards or newsgroups exist in an area of the Internet called Usenet. Here people post messages in public files. You can download these messages to your computer at any time and post a message of your own in response. As with chat rooms, newsgroups exist on countless subjects.

File transfer. On the Internet you can find thousands of files running the gamut from games to virus detectors and everything in between. You can copy or download such files from a remote computer to your computer—usually for free.

 The Internet is changing daily. For updates to this article, visit Houghton Mifflin's Career Planning web site: http://collegesurvival.college.hmco.com/students.

Overcoming technophobia

If you are experiencing technophobia (fear of technology, including computers), then this is a wonderful time to overcome it. You can start with these strategies:

- Get in touch with the benefits of technology. Being comfortable with computers can give you an edge in almost every aspect of being a student, from doing library research to planning your career. In the eyes of many employers, experience with computers is sometimes a necessity and almost always a plus.

- Sign up for a computer class for beginners.

- Ask questions. When it comes to computers, there truly aren't any "dumb" questions.

- Find a competent teacher—someone who remembers what it was like to know nothing about computers.

- Just experiment. Sit down, do something, and see what happens. Short of dropping a computer or hitting it with a hammer, you can't hurt the hardware.

- Remember that computers are not always user-friendly—at least not yet. Learning how to use them takes patience and a lot of time. Knowing this up front can put you at ease and prepare you for the cyberspace adventures ahead.

Finding what you want on the Internet

Imagine a library with millions of books—a place where anyone can bring in materials and place them on any shelf or even toss them randomly on the floor. That's something like the way information accumulates on the Internet. Finding your way through this maze can be a challenge. But it's worth it. On the Internet and at your fingertips are articles on any subject you can imagine, created by individuals and organizations around the planet.

Determine up front what you want.

Before you touch a computer to find something you want on the Internet, know your purpose. You

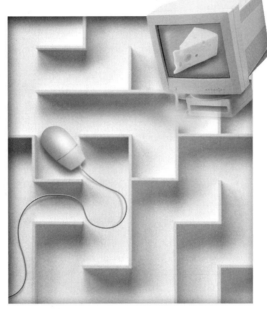

can frame this purpose as a question ("Where can I take a course to prepare for the GMATs?") or a statement ("I want to find the names and addresses of five schools that offer majors in forestry management").

Also consider the *type* of material you want. Perhaps you want statistics, data from a survey, an exact quotation, or the results of a scientific study. In other cases, finding a summary of an article or a feature story from a popular magazine might be all that's needed to meet your purpose.

Use URLs and hyperlinks.

Every document on the Web is identified by a string of letters and numbers called a *URL (Uniform* or *Universal Resource Locator)*. The URL functions as a site's address on the Web. If you have a specific URL on hand, you can type it into your browser and go directly to that document.

When you want to connect to a specific web site, remember to type the URL exactly. Including a stray character or extra space in a URL can send you to an irrelevant web site, just as reversing numbers in a street address can send a letter to the wrong house.

Once you're at the site you want, look for underlined words and phrases that are often in a different color than the rest of the text on the page. These are *hyperlinks* (also called *links*). Clicking on these will take you to related web sites.

Distinguish between directories and search engines.

When searching a nonfiction book for a specific idea or fact, you can use two basic tools. One is the table of contents, a brief ordered list of the major topics in each chapter. The other tool is the index, a detailed alphabetized list of topics and subtopics that appear on each page of the book. When searching the Internet— especially the World Wide Web— you can use similar tools.

Directories offer extensive lists of web pages, all grouped by topic. Think of directories as a table of contents for the Web. Human beings create and maintain these directories, just as librarians create and maintain catalogs of library materials.

Search engines are more like indexes. These tools send out "spiders"—computer programs that "crawl" the Web and other parts of the Internet to find sites that relate to a specific topic. These programs scan millions of web pages in the same way that a human indexer reviews hundreds of book pages.

You'll find sites on the Web that work as either directories or search engines or both. All of these will return a list of web sites that relate to a specific topic.

To use directories and search engines, look for a query box somewhere on the search tool's main page. Move your computer's cursor to that box and type in keywords that relate to the topic you're researching. Say that your purpose is to find a list of mutual funds that invest in bonds offered by the United States Treasury. Keywords relating to your search include *mutual funds*, *bonds*, *treasury*, and *United States*.

The challenge is to get a list of the sites that are most relevant to your purpose. Choosing specific keywords often helps. Whenever possible, use proper nouns and names instead of general concepts or categories.

Go to directories to start your research.

Because these sites are organized by subject, you can often get results that are relevant to your purpose. Go to a search engine later in your research, when you've narrowed down your topic and have more specific keywords.

Find a few search tools you like and use them consistently. That way you get to know each tool well and capitalize on its strengths.

Use Boolean operators.

Boolean operators offer you methods of combining keywords. (These methods were invented by a mathematician named George Boole.) Boolean operators perform a valuable service by helping you narrow your search so that you don't end up with a long list of irrelevant sites.

Boolean operators include the words *AND, OR,* and *NOT.* For example, if you type *portfolios AND résumés,* you'll get a list of web sites that refer to both portfolios and résumés. *Portfolios NOT résumés* will give you sites that relate only to portfolios.

Use other searching tricks.

Knowing some other nifty tricks can help you save even more research time:

- When using a search tool, look for a link that will take you to a page explaining options for doing a more advanced search.
- Restrict your search to a specific part of the Internet, such as newsgroups.
- Bookmark web sites that you frequently visit. (A bookmark is a way to store addresses of sites that you want to visit again.)

Persist.

If you run into a dead end in your research, do at least one more search. Use a new set of keywords or a new search tool. Be persistent. The results you want might be just one click away.

Keep in mind that web sites appear and disappear with surprising frequency. Also, the site that you want might be deluged with more visitors than it can handle. If you can't connect to a site, double-check the URL you're using. Or try connecting again at a later time.

Play.

When you have some time to spare, cultivate serendipity in your searching. Set aside a specific amount of time to surf web sites at random. Have fun. By accident you might stumble on a perfect site to use as a source for your next paper.

Go forth into the world.

Much of the information and ideas created by human beings still doesn't appear on the Internet. This material is stored in academic libraries, public libraries, books, magazines, and newspapers. Some of the information you want might exist only in people's heads. During your research, take a break from the computer and go to the library. Then go into the real world and talk with people. Research is often best done face to face.

EXERCISE

2010 scenario

Write down three possible scenarios describing how the Internet could affect the way you live and work in the year 2010. Choose a best-case scenario, a worst-case scenario, and a most probable case scenario.

Then focus on your most probable case scenario. What could change it into a best-case or worst-case scenario?

_____
_____
_____
_____
_____
_____
_____

Make the information connection— using online resources in career planning

The Internet has changed the world of job hunting from a local concept to a global one. By accessing information online, you can zip a résumé to a company in New York, send an email to request information regarding a position at a firm in San Francisco, and set up an information interview at a company in London—all from the comfort of your own home. Telecommuting has made it possible for people in remote locations to work for large corporations based in metropolitan areas. The Internet also provides a wealth of information about companies and jobs you may not have even considered. *Make the Internet work for you.* To get the most out of online resources, stay open-minded and think critically. Evaluate the source and content carefully.

Find general career information.
Career planning pages abound on the World Wide Web. You'll find scores of sites designed for job hunters. Some sites have career counselors who offer services via email or live chat. Review industry information and salary data and practice your interview skills. Read sample cover letters, learn negotiating skills, and explore articles.

Research employers.
Almost every company has a home page on the Web. These pages can yield vital information about an organization and shine light on its corporate personality. A high-tech web site may indicate a company's dedication to technology and may help you decide whether or not its style fits with yours. Many companies post their annual reports online, a perfect place to read about a company's missions, goals, and accomplishments. Employers often list career opportunities and internships online with a job description, a salary range, benefit information, and a person to contact with questions or to submit your résumé to.

Résumé building and posting.
Some career information web sites offer places for you to build and then post your résumé. These sites allow you to

view résumés other people have posted and to get lists of job openings across the globe. Read posting instructions and requirements carefully so your résumé will print out for a potential employer the same way it prints from your computer. A word of caution: Because your current employer may search for résumés online, you may want to be selective in where you decide to post your résumé.

Cultivate contacts.
This is one area where computers can really help you. Newsgroups, forums, chat rooms, and bulletin boards offer you ways to expand your network and converse with others in real time via your keyboard. Use a search engine to find a group aligned with your career goals.

Download your own library.
Professional journals and organizations post articles, membership information, and event schedules online. You'll find that these types of sites are regularly updated, perfect for helping you stay on top of trends in your field of interest. Consider reading or downloading information. Bookmark your favorite sites and check back often!

Research graduate school programs.
Finding information about new and exciting career opportunities may lead you to seek out additional education classes or degrees. While most schools allow you to request applications and information online, most of the material you need will be posted on their web sites. Review course offerings, degree requirements, and facts about the teaching staff. See if the school you are interested in has a career planning and placement office, and ask questions to help make a decision about a program that fits your needs.

 Begin now. Visit Houghton Mifflin's Career Planning web site for a head start on valuable resources or use a search engine to submit keywords related to your career goals: **http://collegesurvival.college.hmco.com/students.**

PREDICTING TRENDS

Even the most brilliant people can fall flat when predicting trends in business and the workplace. Case in point: Thomas Watson, founder of IBM, said, "I think there's a world market for about five computers."

Still, you can benefit from keeping up-to-date with breaking changes in your career field. That's easier to do than ever before, thanks to resources mentioned throughout this book:

The Internet. Use your skills in searching the Internet to find web sites devoted to your field. Start by keying your job title into a search engine such as Google. Also search for list servers— programs that distribute email messages to groups of people with similar interests.

Periodicals. Read the business sections of the *New York Times* and the *Wall Street Journal*, for example. Many newspapers also have online editions; so do general interest magazines such as *Time* and *Business Week*.

Professional associations. People in similar jobs like to band together and give each other a heads up on emerging trends— one reason for professional associations. These range from the American Medical Association to the Society of Actuaries. There's bound to be one for people in your field. Ask colleagues and search the Internet. *Note:* Many associations post web sites and publish trade magazines.

Conferences and conventions. Many professional associations sponsor annual meetings. Here's where you can meet people face-to-face and use your networking skills. Print and online publications are powerful sources of news, but sometimes nothing beats plain old schmoozing.

[Source for Watson quote: Charles Hard Townes, in Martin Moskovits (Ed.), *Science and Society, the John C. Polanyi Nobel Laureates Lectures*, Anansi Press, Concord, Ontario, 1995, p. 8., listed on *A Dictionary of Scientific Quotations*, http://naturalscience.com/dsqhome.html, accessed 2-6-02]

Thinking critically about information on the Internet

Sources of information on the Internet range from the reputable (such as the Library of Congress) to the flamboyant (such as the *National Enquirer*). This fact underscores the need for thinking critically about every aspect of the Internet.

Long before the Internet, critical thinking was valuable in every form of communication. Typos, mistakes, rumors, and downright lies have crept into print and television throughout the ages. Newspaper, magazine, and book publishers often employ fact checkers, editors, and lawyers to screen out errors and questionable material before publication. But authors of web pages and other Internet sources might not have these resources.

Taking a few simple precautions when you surf the Internet can keep you from crashing onto the rocky shore of misinformation.

Look for overall quality.
Before thinking critically about a web site, step back and examine the features of that site in general. Note the clarity of the text and visuals. Also note how well the site is organized and whether you can navigate the site's features with ease. Look for the date that crucial information was posted, and determine how often the site is updated.

When viewing any web page, you can also evaluate the site's links to related web pages. Look for links to pages of reputable organizations. Click on a few of those links. If they lead you to dead ends, this might indicate a page that's not updated often—one that's not a reliable source for late-breaking information.

Look at the author.
Think about the credibility of the organization that posts a web site. Look for evidence of bias or special interest. Perhaps that organization wants you to buy a service, a product, or a point of view. If so, then determine whether this fact colors the ideas and information posted on the web site. The domain in the Uniform Resource Locator (URL) for a web site can give you significant clues about sources of information and possible bias. For example, distinguish between information from a for-profit enterprise (URL ending in .com), a nonprofit one (.org), a government agency (.gov), and a school, college, or university (.edu).

Distinguish between ideas and information.
To think more powerfully about what you find on the Internet, remember the difference between information and ideas. For example, consider the following sentence: *Nelson Mandela became president of South Africa in 1994.* That statement provides information about South Africa. In contrast, the following sentence states an idea: *Nelson Mandela's presidency means that apartheid has no future in South Africa.*

Information refers to facts that can be verified by independent observers. *Ideas* are interpretations or opinions based on facts. Several people with the same information might adopt different ideas based on that information.

People who speak of the Internet as the "information superhighway" often forget to make this distinction. Don't assume that an idea is reasonable or accurate just because you find it on the Internet.

Look for documentation. When you encounter an assertion on a web page or other Internet resource, note the types and quality of the evidence offered. Look for credible examples, quotations from authorities in the field, documented statistics, or summaries of scientific studies. Also look for endnotes, bibliographies, or another way to find the original sources of information.

Set an example. In the midst of the Internet's chaotic growth, you can light a path of rationality. Whether you're sending a short email message or building a massive web site, you can bring your own critical thinking skills into play. Every word and image you send down the wires to the Web can display the hallmarks of critical thinking—sound logic, credible evidence, and respect for your audience.

 You can find additional suggestions for thinking critically about information on the Internet at Houghton Mifflin's Career Planning web site: **http://collegesurvival.college. hmco.com/students.**

The changing workforce

As a 21st-century worker, you'll need flexibility and creativity to survive in a workplace that is constantly changing and advancing. What worked in the 1900s will not work in the 2000s, and the workforce in 5, 10, or 20 years will undoubtedly be very different from what it is now. Notice how workers of the past (Industrial Age workers) compare to workers of today (Information Age workers).

Industrial Age Workers	Information Age Workers
Depend on supervisor	Assume personal responsibility; shared leadership
Listen	Communicate
Follow orders	Make decisions; solve problems
Compete (personal power)	Cooperate (shared goals)
Product-oriented (factory)	Process- or people-oriented (global)
Follow routines (security)	Innovative (risk-taking)
Boss-oriented	Team-oriented
Highly defined job	Project-based assignments
Information filters down from management	Information received directly, frequently, online
Rule-bound; slow	Flexible; responsive
"Tell me what to do"	"Here's what I can do"
Resistant to change	Constantly learning

Amidst all the changes, however, remember that critical thinking skills don't change. They adapt well to a changing work environment and help you to meet the challenges of a fast-moving, competitive careers. Notice how relevant critical thinking is when you're actually on the job.

Return to the key player—YOU

As you research careers, you may find yourself swimming in information about the world of work—stacks of figures, facts, names, and job titles.

There is a way out. Keep in mind that data is different from insight. Data about the work world is not useful until it's poured through a filter—you. The following suggestions can help in matching job data with your interests, skills, and values.

Focus on a general field first

Field is another word for a group of related jobs. For example, doctors, nurses, and medical lab technicians all work in health care, the same field.

Finding lists of fields can help when you haven't narrowed down your search to a specific job. You can just keep gathering information about a whole. For instance, if your passion is entertaining people, you can research specific jobs in this field. Examples are musician, comedian, nightclub owner, and actor. At this point, there is no need to unduly limit your research. You can just bask in the field for a while.

Consider the people and environment

As workers, we are social animals. Any job takes place around people. What's more, each job takes place in a physical space—anything from a church to a rock-and-roll club.

To get an accurate picture of any career you're considering, ask whom you might work with and where. It's possible you could love working on cars but not enjoy spending 40 hours a week at a gas station. Gain such information before choosing a career.

Remember the data by building a structure

You can organize your career information into a simple structure. For example, the process of career planning can be "mapped" according to the steps used in this book—commit, dream, discover yourself, discover work, plan, act, and celebrate.

You can also build a structure by going through a list of questions as you encounter new information. Sample questions:

- How current is this information?
- What is the source of information?
- How important is this information to me?
- How useful do I think this idea will be?
- How favorably do I respond to this idea?
- How well suited is this idea to my interests, abilities, and values?

Forget the data

To cope with complexity, forget the data once in a while. Turn to something other than career planning. Take a nap. Ride a bike. Listen to music. Do anything to change the pace and renew yourself. While your conscious mind is relaxing, another part of your mind will store, sort, and interpret all your career research.

The ideas that result from this process may seem to come from out of the blue—an image in your dreams, a flash of insight while you're taking a shower, a sudden "Aha!" experience while you're waiting for a bus. Suddenly you might see a pattern in the data, a meaning behind all the facts. From such experiences can emerge an enduring career choice.

JOURNAL ENTRY

Discovery/Intention Statement

Choose one career field to find out more about. List your choice here:

_____

_____

_____

Next, choose three jobs within this field that interest you. To complete this step, you may want to do some research, using the resources mentioned in this chapter. Find out enough about each job to answer these questions:

Does this job deal mostly with people? With things? With data and ideas?

Does this job call for skills that I value and would enjoy using? Which skills?

Write your answers on 3×5 cards or on a separate sheet of paper.

Then complete the following sentences:

The job in the field that sounds most interesting to me is …

_____

_____

_____

_____

In the next 10 days, I will learn more about this career or job by taking these three kinds of action:

1. _____

_____

_____

_____

_____

2. _____

_____

_____

_____

3. _____

_____

_____

_____

_____

1 List five resources for finding out more about the world of work.

2 This chapter suggests several ways to jump into the world of work. Describe four of them.

3 What are three important questions to ask during an information interview?

4 Name two places available to you where you can upgrade your computer skills.

5 Aside from looking for a specific position on the Internet, name two useful ways the Web can work for you.

Plan

Creativity involves breaking out of established patterns in order to look at things in a different way.
EDWARD DE BONO

Goals are dreams with deadlines.
DIANA SCHARF HUNT

IN THIS CHAPTER . . . If you want to be free, plan. Planning creates new options and makes daily decisions easier. Brainstorm some possible plans. Be creative. Prioritize your goals. Adding time lines, priorities, categories, and domains can increase the odds of meeting your goals. Create a career plan in a visual format.

If you want to be free, plan

When you plan anything—including your career—you create freedom. One value of planning your career is that you gain skill in planning any other aspect of your life as well.

This idea contrasts with the common fear of planning: "Me? Plan? No way. I don't want to be uptight. I don't want to be restrained. I want to be free."

Great. Then plan.

"No, no," goes the reply. "If I plan, I'll be trapped. I won't be able to just let loose and have a good time. I'll be boxed in by this plan."

Actually, one path to freedom is planning. One path to feeling calm, peaceful, fun-loving, joyful, and powerful is to have a plan. When people are uptight, worried, and hassled—when they're not feeling free—they often have no plan.

You set the plan

One freedom in planning stems from the simple fact that you set the plan. The course and direction of your life are yours.

Often, particularly at work or in school, people do not feel this way. They think the plan is coming from someone else—their employer, supervisor, or teacher.

Consider that this view is inaccurate. When we look far enough in advance, we discover that the overall direction is still our own. The power of a career plan is being able to step back and say, "I choose to see my present job or my present circumstance as part of a plan for my whole life. When I see far enough in advance, my present job no longer feels limiting. And even when I don't like parts of my current job, I gain income and develop skills for a new job."

You can change the plan

Another freedom in planning is freedom to change. An effective plan is flexible, ready to be altered at any moment.

Tell people that you have a 20-year plan for your career. They might ask, "Well, if the economy changes, would you consider changing your plan?" "Yes," you reply. "I change it every year." Then comes the laughter: "Well it really isn't a 20-year plan if you change it every year. It's actually a one-year plan."

As our lives change, we can change our plans. In fact, we can change our plans often and still preserve all the advantages of planning. Those advantages come from constantly aligning our current activities with our core values.

You choose how to achieve the plan

Planning increases freedom as it creates choices. Suppose you take a new job, and with it comes a detailed list of goals to achieve in one year. You might say, "I have no freedom. I didn't choose these goals. I guess I'll just have to put up with them."

There is another option. Even when others select the goals, you can decide whether to accept them. You can also choose many different paths to a goal. You can still ask: What are my options for achieving this goal? Do I take this route or another route? This action or another? There is tremendous freedom in such questions.

When there's a plan, there's a chance

Planning makes it much more likely that we'll reach our goals. We have a plan. We've laid out the necessary actions in logical steps. And we've chosen a time to perform each action. Now a goal seems possible where perhaps it seemed impossible before.

Much of what people undertake at work, in relationships, and at home is simply "digging in"—frantic action with no plan. Planning replaces that despair with a purpose and a timeline.

Planning frees you from constant decisions

When we operate without a plan, we may change our minds often. This kind of change is often a knee-jerk reaction. Sometimes it involves a lengthy internal debate: "Hmmmm . . . . That chocolate cake smells great. Maybe I'll have a piece—but maybe I shouldn't. It's a lot of calories. I don't know. . . ." Such a debate takes up a lot of time and energy.

Suppose you simply plan to stop eating chocolate cake. What's more, you write down this plan, speak the plan to friends, and even commit to this plan in their presence. Then you're free from a new decision every time you see a piece of chocolate cake. The same strategy works for larger goals, such as your choice of career.

Planning makes adjustments easier

With a plan, you're free to handle unexpected change. Suppose you are scheduled to give a talk in your speech class next week. Suddenly you find out there was a misprint in the course schedule. You're supposed to speak two days from now, not seven. Without a plan, you could face a whole series of decisions: What will I do now? When will I have time to get that speech done? How will this affect the rest of my schedule?

With a plan, things are different. You can say, "I don't have to worry about this. I've done my plan for the week, and I know I have free time tomorrow night between 7 and 10 p.m. I can finish the speech then."

With a written plan, we can make such comparisons quickly. Without a plan, we are often bounced around, passively responding to unexpected events.

Planning is about creating our own experience. Moment by moment we make choices, and the sum of these choices is our present situation. When we plan, our situation does not just "happen" to us. Instead, it follows from choices we've consciously made for ourselves. This self-direction is a fundamental freedom in planning—and one of the most valued freedoms of all.

EXERCISE

Experience the benefits of planning

During the next week, observe how you spend your time during one unplanned day. At the end of that day, list what you did during each one-hour time block in those 24 hours. Next, choose one day in the following week and write a fairly detailed plan for the day. Focus on an eight-hour block of time, and note how you intend to spend each hour. When the day comes, follow your plan as closely as possible.

Then compare your planned day with your unplanned day. For best results, compare similar days of the week—Mondays with Mondays, Saturdays with Saturdays. In the space below, list any benefits you experienced in planning.

_____

_____

_____

_____

Choose one benefit you just listed. Then complete the following sentence: I intend to make this benefit a part of my daily life by taking these actions:

_____

_____

_____

_____

7 Ways to Stop Procrastination

Observe your procrastination. Instead of rushing to fix your procrastination problem, take your time. Get to know your problem well. Avoid judgments. Clearly seeing the cost of procrastination can help you kick the habit.

Discover your procrastination style. Awareness of procrastination styles is a key to changing your behavior. For example, if you exhibit the characteristics of an overdoer, then say no to new projects. Also ask for help in getting your current projects done.

Look for self-defeating beliefs. Certain thoughts fuel procrastination and keep you from experiencing the rewards in life that you deserve.

Getting a belief out of your head and onto paper can rob that belief of its power. Also write a more effective belief that you want to adopt. For example: "Even if I don't complete this task perfectly, it's good enough for now and I can still learn from my mistakes."

Trick yourself into getting started. Practice being a con artist—and your own unwitting target. If you have a 50-page chapter to read, grab the book and say to yourself, "I'm not really going to read this chapter right now. I'm just going to flip through the pages and scan the headings for 10 minutes." Tricks like these can get you started at a task you've been dreading. Once you get started, you might find it easy to keep going.

Let feelings follow action. If you put off exercising until you feel energetic, you might wait for months. Instead, get moving now and watch your feelings change. After five minutes of brisk walking, you might be in the mood for a 20-minute run. This principle—action generates motivation—can apply to any task that's been delegated to the back burner.

Choose to work under pressure. Sometimes people thrive under pressure. As one writer put it, "I don't do my *best* work because of a tight timeline. I do my *only* work with a tight timeline." Used selectively, this strategy might also work for you.

Take it easy. You can find shelves full of books with techniques for overcoming procrastination. Make one small, simple change in behavior—today. Tomorrow, make the change again. Take it day by day until the new behavior becomes a habit. One day you might wake up and discover that procrastination is part of your past.

EXERCISE

Create a lifeline

 An online version of this exercise is available at Houghton Mifflin's Career Planning web site: **http://collegesurvival. college.hmco.com/students.**

On a large sheet of paper, draw a horizontal line. This line will represent your lifetime. Now add key events in your life to this line in chronological order. Examples are birth, first day at school, graduation from high school, and enrollment in higher education.

Now extend the lifeline into the future. Write down key events you would like to see occur in 1 year, 5 years, and 10 years or more from now. Choose events that align with your core values. Work quickly in the spirit of a brainstorm. This is not a final plan.

Afterward, take a few minutes to review your lifeline. Select one key event for the future and list any actions you could take in the next month to bring yourself closer to that goal. Do the same with other key events on your lifeline. You now have the rudiments of a comprehensive plan for your life.

Finally, extend your lifeline another 50 years beyond the year when you would reach age 100. Describe in detail what changes in the world you'd like to see as a result of the goals you attained in your lifetime.

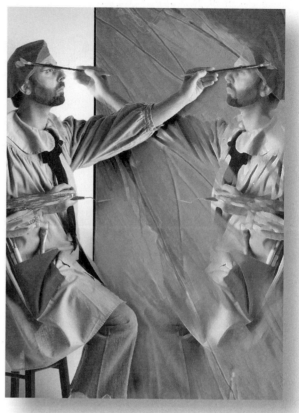

Planning by creation

For most people, the word *planning* means almost the same as *prediction.* Actually, there's another option, one called *planning by creation.* Using this option can change your whole experience of creating your career—and your life.

Much of the goal setting that's done today in business, government, and education is planning by prediction. In this type of planning, people carefully study what's happened in the past and use the data to predict what will happen in the future.

Assumptions underlie planning

Planning by prediction is based on a few assumptions. One is that past events are the best predictors of what's yet to come. Another is that the forces now shaping our lives will continue to be at work in the future. In a sense, prediction is the past masquerading as the future.

Planning by creation involves a different set of working assumptions. With this second type of planning,

we start with a clean slate—with nothing. Without considering the past, we state what we want to happen in the future. Then we ask how to achieve those goals. The underlying idea is that the past does not have to limit what can happen in the future.

This is not to say that planning by creation is "better" than planning by prediction. Both types of planning are valid. Both have their uses. The point is to know at any given moment what kind of planning you're doing and to choose the type that suits your purpose.

An example: Two ways to create a budget

To understand the differences between planning by prediction and planning by creation, look at two ways to create a budget.

For many companies, budgeting is an example of planning by prediction. Corporate planners predict next year's income and expenses on the basis of this year's income and expenses.

An alternative is creating a budget from scratch. This means taking last year's budget, crumpling it up, and throwing it away. Instead of fixing last year's figures, planners can ask a lot of questions: What do we value? What do we want to be doing one year from now? How much money do we want to be making? How much do we want to be spending? And what steps can we take to meet these goals?

Sometimes this approach is called *zero-based budgeting*. The same process could be applied to many areas of life and called *zero-based planning*—or planning by creation.

Prediction is risky

When planning by creation, we acknowledge that prediction is risky business. Most of us—even tea leaf readers and crystal ball gazers—are not skilled at predicting the future. People who read the *Wall Street Journal* every day can still lose on the stock market. Political pundits can err when predicting the outcome of an election.

In planning by creation, we bypass these risks. Our aim is not to *predict* the future but to *shape* it. We think about the changes we want to see in our lives, our communities, our world. We imagine the new results we could generate, even if they'll take 5, 10, 20, or more years to achieve.

One way to plan by creation

The following steps can get you started with planning by creation.

Step 1: Begin with a clean slate

As you prepare to create your future, be willing to completely let go of your past and current circumstances. Instead of looking at history, erase history.

For this step, pretend that you have all the time, money, and resources you could ever want. Then ask: What do I want to be in the future? What do I want to do? What do I want to have?

As you ask these questions, ignore the voices that say, "You've never done anything like that." "No one has ever done that before." "People have always said that couldn't be done." Instead of allowing the past to place limits on you, let your imagination soar. Allow yourself to literally create the future from nothing.

Step 2: Design the future

Now, in your mind's eye, see yourself in the future. Describe the conditions you'd like to see in your career, family, or community 20 or more years from today.

The trick is to speak about those conditions as if they exist right now. Describe in detail what you're doing, seeing, and feeling as you stand in the future. Let those events be dynamic, multidimensional, and ever-changing.

For example, say that your overall goal is to work in careers that eliminate world hunger. You could begin with this vision:

I'm standing in Ethiopia in the year 2100. As I look around, I see that there's plenty of food for everybody. Starvation, famine, and malnutrition are all things of the past. The land is lush and green. There's plenty of clean water to go around. The children are well fed and healthy, running from house to house, laughing and playing, and they go to well-furnished schools with dedicated, patient teachers.

Step 3: Describe the present

Like the future, the present is dynamic and multidimensional. With this in mind, describe the present as it relates to your preferred future.

To get the most out of this step, be honest. Tell the truth about the present. If your design for the future includes a world free of starvation, then freely and fully admit how many people are dying of hunger today.

Step 4: Link the future to the present

Now create mid-range goals that work "backward" from the future to the present. As you do so, continue to mentally dwell in the future. In fact, assume that your preferred future has already been achieved.

Say that you envisioned the world you'd like to see in the year 2500. Now imagine what happened in the year 2400 that allowed that world to come to pass. Do the same for the years 2300, 2200, 2100.... Continue this process until you reach the present.

Return to the example of Ethiopia. To link that compelling future to the present, you could create intermediate steps like the following:

I'm in the year 2100—the year that the problem of irrigating arid lands in this country was finally solved....

It's now 2050. A new technology that transformed this country's system of dams and reservoirs is finally in place. This technology allows farmers to stockpile water between droughts....

Now we're in the present time. We've learned ways to desalinate water from the ocean and make it available to farmers across the continent of Africa. This discovery holds the promise to transform the way food is grown and distributed.

Notice that this process is the exact opposite of planning by prediction. When most people set goals, they start in the present and work forward in time. In creating the future from nothing, you start at the future and work backward in time toward the present.

If you observe children at play, you may notice them doing this kind of creation. In their make-believe worlds, children spin fantasies, unhampered for the moment by any "practical" questions about ways to make those fantasies come true. As you experiment with planning by creation, allow yourself to regain that sense of childlike wisdom.

Plan to be satisfied with your solution

Once you've decided to plan by creation, you can study what's happened in the past and use this information to predict the future. Before you can determine what type of company you would like to work for, a first step may include doing research. Check on what your potential employer has created in the past, and begin to envision its plans for the future. Information about a company's presence and corporate culture can be found online. Observing their site and reading information can help you to look towards *your* place as an employee with this company.

There's no place like home

Start with the company's homepage. Look for clues here? for starters, check out when this page was last updated. This will help you to determine the company's commitment to technology. Since visiting their homepage helps to provide a first impression, notice what you like and what elements have room for improvement. Keep these ideas

in mind if you end up at an interview with this company. Talking about what you learned about the company while investigating their site can help you show an employer your level of interest and your creativity.

Start your engine

Find out about current events and how they relate to a potential employer by running the company name into a search engine (like Yahoo or Google). Because a company's web site may not focus on changes in personnel or earnings for the last quarter, using multiple resources like a homepage and a search engine, can provide you with the big picture. Doing your research will help you target the best potential employer. Visit other career sites (like Vault or Monster) that have "insider" information about companies and industry trends to assist you in your research.

Follow through

Whether you are doing research or interviewing for a job, following through with your plan by taking action will help you accomplish your career goals. Assess yourself at different steps in the planning process, like the journal entries in this book help you do. After you've done your research, think about how you might re-create your career plan. Whether you choose a different company to send your resume to or you change your career goals altogether, you are in charge.

 Visit Houghton Mifflin's Career Planning web site to read the article "The Five Minute Super Creativity Tool" for more ideas: http://collegesurvival.college.hmco.com/students.

EXERCISE

Create your future from nothing

This exercise is an open inquiry as to what's possible for the rest of your life ... and beyond. During this exercise, you will experiment with totally erasing your current personal identity—that is, starting your life over again. After that, you will set goals for your career and other aspects of your life.

Be willing to stick with this process even if it sounds crazy. There is a logic hidden in this exercise. Most of us live full lives, filled with a lot of "something." We carry around a detailed personal history: successes, failures, attachments, requirements, relationships, careers, thoughts, feelings, habits, and much more.

All this history serves a purpose. At the same time, we can become so committed to preserving our history that we squash any possibility of personal change. Our lives can get so "full" that we leave no room for something fresh—like a room that is so full of furniture that it has no place for a beautiful new painting.

So consider what it would be like to re-create your life from a clean slate. Imagine that you could wipe out the past and start over fresh. What would you do? What would you have? Who should you choose to be?

If all this sounds frightening, remember that you don't have to physically give up anything. This exercise is just that— a mental exploration.

To begin with a blank state, experiment with the following suggestions:

- Erase your current job. Imagine that you have no job. Whether you love it or hate it, or feel neutral about it, the job's gone. Vanished. (Relax. You can have your job back at the end of this exercise.)

- Erase your financial concerns. Money problems are permanently behind you. In fact, imagine that money is no longer used as a medium of exchange. Banks and credit cards no longer exist. There's no point in having money, and no one has any. Money is gone.

- Erase your health problems. Disease, chronic illness, or disability are no longer barriers for you.

- Erase your friends. Peers, colleagues, neighbors, acquaintances—all of them are gone. Don't worry about being lonely. You can make more friends later.

- Erase your enemies. Imagine that any people you resented or fought with are no longer part of your life.

- Erase your family. Again don't worry. These people are safe, and you can bring them back later. For now, however, pretend that they are no longer around.

- Erase your spouse or romantic partner. Do this now, even if you have a wonderful relationship. Let this person go to the same place where your friends and family have gone.

- Erase your house or apartment. As for now, imagine that you have no place to live. No longer do you define yourself by the size, price, or location of your living space.

- Erase your other possessions, especially the big-ticket items such as cars or boats.

- Erase the community where you live. The town, city, or rural area where you grew up is gone. So is the place where you lived until you read this exercise.

- Erase your memories. All those accomplishments, those hurts, those mistakes—release them all.

- Erase your watch. As you mentally toss your timepiece out the window, also erase any awareness of time.

- Now notice anything about yourself that remains. Is your body still there? Erase it. Are your clothes or glasses still there? Erase them, too. (Notice that we erased your body before we erased your clothes; no need to feel embarrassed.) Also erase your emotions, opinions, and thoughts. If you have any worry about all that you've erased so far, just notice that worry and let go of it also. Then erase anything that's left.

- Finally, notice any remaining thoughts about this exercise— that it's silly, profound, boring, frightening, or anything else. Let those thoughts billow up and vanish like a bubble.

If these suggestions worked for you, you're probably at a blank state. Congratulations. You've arrived at a peak state of creativity. In fact, now that you're nobody, you may even be better company than when you were merely somebody. At this moment, you're free to make any choice whatsoever about what to be, do, and have. From the state of nothingness, you can call forth all possibilities.

Dwell in this state for just a little while longer. As you do, ask yourself, What do I want in my career and any other areas of my life? Express your answers as goals written on 3x5 cards.

After you've recorded these goals, slowly let yourself start to fill up again. Allow all your old roles and possessions to gradually rejoin you. Return yourself to the present.

When you've fully come back to the present, review the goals you wrote just a few minutes ago—back when you were nothing.

Four paths to more powerful goals

Doing the exercises in this book probably left you with a large stack of possible career goals, perhaps hundreds of them. Now it's time to gather all those ideas, refine them, and include them in a complete draft of your career plan.

To enhance the power of your goals, consider rewriting each of them on a 3x5 card or on your computer. In addition, you can add any of the following items next to your goal:

- Priority
- Timeline
- Category
- Domain

Add priorities

Not all the goals you create will be equally important. Accomplishing some of them will create more value for you than accomplishing others. In order to get the most out of your efforts, assign priorities.

There are several options. *Letters of the alphabet* offer a tried-and-true way to assign priorities. A common method is the ABC system. Here, the most important and urgent goals receive an A rating, less urgent and unimportant goals become B's and the mere possibilities are rated as C's.

Another method of prioritizing is simple *rank ordering*. You number goals in order of their importance.

Goal number 1 is the one you'll work toward first, followed by goal number 2, goal number 3, and so on.

You can also assign priority with *words*. For example, each of the following phrases signals a level of priority, going from lowest to highest:

- "I *might* accomplish this goal."
- "I *want* to accomplish this goal."
- "I *plan* to accomplish this goal."
- "I *promise* to accomplish this goal."

A fourth option is to use *numbers*. For example, rate each goal on a scale from 1 to 100. Goals numbered 1 to 30 can be possibilities (C priorities). Goals in the 31 to 60 range can be plans (B priorities), and those numbered 61 to 100 can be promises (A priorities).

Add timelines

Choose due dates for major goals. Adding a timeline to your goals is one way to raise your level of commitment. Many people report that when they add timelines, their goals suddenly become more concrete and attainable.

You can use several options for stating timelines. Some examples:

"I will achieve this goal by (date)."

"I will do this until (date)."

"I will do this from (date) to (date)."

Note that a goal without a timeline can still be powerful. Some goals are more effective with no timeline at all. That's true of "be loving" or "practice forgiveness." You probably wouldn't want to limit such goals with a timeline. ("I will be loving on Tuesday afternoons." "I will practice forgiveness until I turn 50.")

You might feel stumped when choosing a timeline. No problem. If you're in doubt, just pick a date or range of dates out of the air. And if the timeline looks off-base once you write it down, then just change it.

Add categories

Before you feel overwhelmed by the sheer number of your goals, take a few minutes to create a list of five to seven major categories for them. Then sort your goals into the categories.

No one list of categories makes sense for everyone. Choose a set of topics that works for you. Some examples are these:

- Opportunities for promotion
- Skills to develop
- Professional contacts
- Education
- Experience
- People to contact
- People already contacted

Add domains

We can also label our goals as part of three domains: *Be, do,* or *have.* By distinguishing the domain of the goal, we can begin to balance, the number of goals we put into each of these areas.

People generally create most of their goals in the domain of *have.* These goals are about circumstances and things we'd like to own. Examples include these: "I want to have more money." "I plan to have a new house." "I want to have a cure for cancer."

Have goals represent only one possible domain for goals. A second domain is action—*do* goals. These name actions that we plan to take. Here are examples: "I want to exercise three times per week." "I plan to enter graduate school." "I want to travel to Europe." "I will write 100 words per day in my journal."

A third domain for goals has to do with values—*be* goals. Possible goals in this area are these: "I will be more loving." "I want to be more frugal." "I will be spontaneous."

Many plans focus primarily on results or circumstances—what people want to have. Who we *are* and what we typically *do* are just as important to consider. Achieving a balance in all three domains—having, doing, and being—can make for a more comprehensive, effective plan.

Do what works

The suggestions to list priorities, timelines, categories, and domains are just that—suggestions. You might choose to let some goals stand without any one of these elements. Add the four elements explained in this article when they help clarify your thinking and move you into action.

Above all, keep creating goals. You can come back later to add a priority, timeline, category, or domain when appropriate.

Motivation—it's within you

Motivation can come simply from being clear about your goals and acting on them. Practice being motivated and disciplined like you would develop a habit. Try these suggestions to help get you started.

Promise it. Say that you want to start a list of people to network with. You can commit yourself to making a list and sending out an email to make contact with these people. Promise yourself that you'll do this and hold yourself accountable.

Ask for support. Other people can become your allies in overcoming procrastination. For example, form a career planning support group and declare what you intend to accomplish before each meeting. Then ask members to hold you accountable.

Compare the payoffs to the costs. One way to let go of unwanted behaviors is first to celebrate them? Even embrace them. This can be especially powerful when we follow it up with the next step—Determining the costs. For example, not visiting a company's web site before an interview can give you time to go to the movies. However, you might be unprepared in an interview if a question is asked about what section you liked best on a company's web site. With some thoughtful weekly planning, you might choose to give up a few hours of television and end up with enough time to do both.

Turn up the pressure. Sometimes motivation is a luxury. Pretend that the due date for your project has been moved up one month, one week or one day. Raising the stress level slightly can spur you into action. Then the issue of motivation seems beside the point, and meeting the due date moves to the forefront.

Fine-tune your career plan

Skilled writers are seldom done with an article or book when they finish a first draft. Revising their drafts gives writers more opportunities to sharpen word choice, delete unnecessary sentences, and fix gaps in logic.

Likewise, revising the first draft of your goals can make them more complete, specific, and focused—and thereby easier to meet.

Add more details

Give your goals more "juice" by infusing them with details. To do so, answer some of these questions about many of your goals:

- What specific outcome do I want?
- When will I accomplish this goal?
- Where will I accomplish this goal?
- Who can help me accomplish this goal?
- What are some possible obstacles to meeting this goal?
- How can I overcome those obstacles?

Check for alignment

Take a break to step back and look for overall consistency in your goals. See if your goals are aligned with each other and with your values. If a person who values frugality also has a goal to own 50 pairs of shoes, that's a sign of goal conflict. This kind of contradiction can muddle our thinking and lead to confused action.

Translate goals into other media

When reviewing your written goals, you can translate them into a more visual, nonverbal form, such as a chart, diagram, or other graphic. Use colors. Draw pictures. Or create in three dimensions by building scale models, as architects do. These are just a few of the possibilities.

Let your format be unique

Your vision of the future does not have to look like anyone else's. There is no official format for any set of goals. One person's vision of the future might consist of a box of 3×5 cards, sorted by categories. Someone else might prefer a formal written document. Others might choose a computer database program that can sort and display goals in many formats. More possibilities exist.

Choosing a format for your goals is one way to let your creativity flourish. Experiment and find a format that works for you. Any structure that clarifies your preferred future and moves you into action is fine.

JOURNAL ENTRY

Discovery/Intention Statement

Making revisions to your goals and career plan is an important part of the process of career planning. Brainstorming new and creative ideas will help you make this your own. Take 5 minutes and think about ways in which you could improve upon your plan using your creativity. What would you do first to change your current plan? Think outside of the box.

_____

_____

_____

EXERCISE

Ask someone else to plan your career

One creativity technique that can lead to outrageous fun is the practice of planning another person's life.

If this sounds like a call to violate someone's privacy, consider that people set goals for each other all the time. Teachers set goals for their students. Parents set goals for their children. Salespeople set goals for their customers, and employers set goals for their employees.

Setting goals for others can actually promote their happiness and freedom. And it's always up to others whether to accept our goals.

With these thoughts in mind, invite another person to brainstorm goals for you. Ask this person, "If you were going to live my life, what would you do, have, and be?"

Let the other person speak for 10 minutes while you take notes, recording suggested goals. Remember that you can keep all the other person's ideas, use only a few of them, or throw them all away after this exercise is done.

To get the most out of this exercise, listen without judgment. Reacting defensively defeats the purpose, which is to practice creative thinking. This kind of thinking flourishes in an atmosphere of total candor and detachment. If you hear a goal that confuses or angers you, just notice your reaction. Then return your attention to listening.

EXERCISE

Add details to your plan

Review the goals you've set so far. Consider adding the following items to each one.

- A rating of priority
- A timeline (due date) for the goal
- A category under which you'll file this goal
- A domain of this goal (*be, do,* or *have*)

Sample formats for career plans

Following are excerpts from career plans in several different formats:

Sample #1: A timeline that marks dates for major career events in the future. (This timeline is also called a "lifeline.")

Sample #2: A mind map that links personal values to desired skills that could be used in several careers.

Sample #3: A pie chart summarizing the amounts of time devoted to career-related activities. A sample pie chart is shown on page 79.

Sample #4: A list of career goals sorted by priority. In this case, each goal is assigned a number from 1 to 100. Higher numbers denote higher priority.

You can review these samples for useful ideas. Your career plan can combine any of these formats—and others that you create.

Also be sure to keep in mind the format for planning explained throughout this chapter: writing individual goals on 3×5 cards and storing those cards in a file box with card dividers.

SAMPLE #1: Timeline

Note: The following timeline could also include dates for events related to family life, recreation, and other areas of life. Also notice that this person's timeline includes a date 100 years into the future. His plan is to take part in projects that will go well beyond his death.

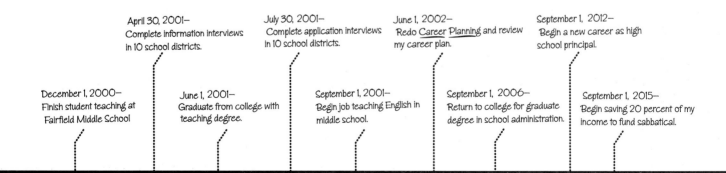

April 30, 2001—
Complete information interviews in 10 school districts.

July 30, 2001—
Complete application interviews in 10 school districts.

June 1, 2002—
Redo Career Planning and review my career plan.

September 1, 2012—
Begin a new career as high school principal.

December 1, 2000—
Finish student teaching at Fairfield Middle School

June 1, 2001—
Graduate from college with teaching degree.

September 1, 2001—
Begin job teaching English in middle school.

September 1, 2006—
Return to college for graduate degree in school administration.

September 1, 2015—
Begin saving 20 percent of my income to fund sabbatical.

SAMPLE #2: Mind map

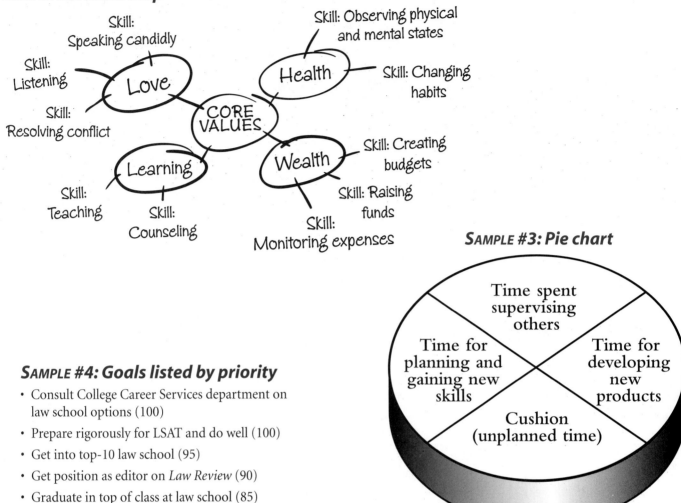

SAMPLE #3: Pie chart

SAMPLE #4: Goals listed by priority

- Consult College Career Services department on law school options (100)
- Prepare rigorously for LSAT and do well (100)
- Get into top-10 law school (95)
- Get position as editor on *Law Review* (90)
- Graduate in top of class at law school (85)
- Work for state district attorney's office (80)
- Use my position and influence to gain political and judicial contacts (75)
- Found private law firm focused on protection of workers' rights (70)
- Win major lawsuits in defense of individual liberties in the workplace (60)
- Leave law practice to travel to Third World countries in aid of poor for two years (60)
- Found international agency in protection of human rights (50)
- Win Nobel Prize (30)

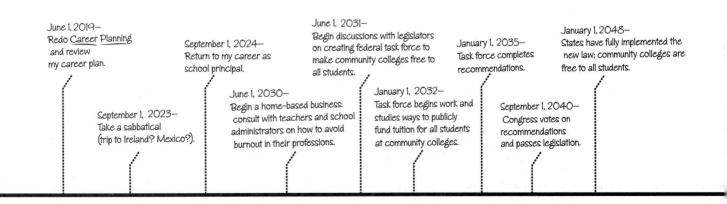

Name _____ Date _____/_____/_____

Choose now

If you have not already done so, choose a career field—right here, right now. Remember that nothing about it is final. You can change your mind in five years, five months, five days, or five minutes. For now, just choose a career.

Your choice can be in a broad field that still gives you room to pursue many different jobs. For example, someone who chooses education as a field can consider job titles including those of teacher, counselor, principal, instructional designer, curriculum consultant, Internet architect, and many more.

Complete the following sentence:

The career I choose is …

_____
_____
_____
_____
_____
_____
_____
_____
_____
_____
_____
_____
_____
_____
_____
_____
_____
_____
_____
_____
_____
_____
_____
_____
_____
_____
_____

1 Briefly describe how planning can create freedom.

2 A plan that changes often is not a useful plan. True or False? Explain your answer.

3 Summarize the differences between planning by prediction and planning by creation.

4 How can assigning priorities help you to accomplish your goals?

5 Which format best suits your style for diagramming your career plan? Explain your answer.

*Challenges make
you discover things
about yourself that
you never really knew.
They're what make the
instrument stretch—
what makes you go
beyond the norm.*
DAVID BOREN

*Overcoming your inertia
and acting will give you
a whole new lease on
being creatively alive.*
WAYNE DYER

IN THIS CHAPTER ... Use power tools for finding work. Reconsider traditional strategies for job hunting. Translate goals into action. Brainstorm a list of actions you could take in the next week to help yourself achieve those goals. Build your own network. Create a résumé that will help you land a job. Write powerful cover letters and thank-you notes. Plan your answers to résumé questions.

Use power tools for finding work

TOOL #1: Upgrade your strategies

When applied to finding work, not all strategies are equal. People often find their job searches less effective when they do the following things:

- Rely exclusively on want ads when looking for a job.

- Mail out a stack of résumés and cover letters and simply wait for a reply.

- Wait for a job to open up before contacting potential employers.

- Work only with employment agencies and human resources departments in large companies.

- Rely on an interview as their only source of information about an employer.

These methods are not all useless. Rather, problems arise when we rely on just one strategy and exclude others.

As an alternative, consider the following ideas based on employment research, suggestions from career counselors, and the experience of job hunters. They can greatly increase your chances of getting the job you want:

- Make direct contact with a person who can hire you.

- Make such contacts even when the job you want is not yet open or even conceived.

- Cultivate a list of contacts, join professional associations, and meet people in your field.

- Approach a potential employer with a way to solve a problem or achieve a company goal. Talk about what's in it for her—the benefits to the company if you are hired.

- Do thorough research on a company before approaching someone for a job there. Do part of this research via information interviews.

- Follow up a résumé with letters and well-timed phone calls.

- Write thank-you notes after an interview.

- Have an impeccable presentation. This includes everything from résumés that are free of grammatical errors to dressing well and polishing your shoes.

TOOL #2: Consider more than one career

When you begin career planning, consider many options. Doing so increases your flexibility over the long term. Also avoid specializing in a certain field too soon, or becoming so specialized that it's difficult to find work as the market changes.

As an alternative, keep an overall perspective. Use your education to learn how different ideas and jobs are interconnected. Look for the common threads that unite subjects and careers.

TOOL #3: Keep a portfolio or record of achievements

Students preparing for careers in the arts often keep samples of their work on hand. These might include paintings, sculptures, slides, tapes, or photographs. They use such samples when applying for teaching positions or grants, for instance.

Even if you're not in the arts, you can begin a portfolio. Journalism students can keep examples of their writing. Students majoring in computer science can keep copies of programs they've written. Any anyone who works can keep a journal of accomplishments on the job.

Tool #4: Develop interests, skills, and friends different from those in your career

You might find it refreshing to learn about yourself outside the context of your job or major. To do this, break out of ruts. Be creative and be open to new activities. Take a course that has nothing to do with your major or career. Volunteer. Invest time and energy in the lives of others. Besides infusing our lives with a new perspective, such activity can open us to new career possibilities.

Tool #5: Use spare minutes

Career planning and job hunting give you a way to wring value out of every spare moment. The time you spend waiting in line at the bank, at the laundromat, or at the gas station never needs to be wasted again. Many career-planning and job-hunting tasks can be done in one hour or less.

In fact, there's a lot you can do in five minutes. One option is to take a five-minute career-planning break. Fill that break with "microtasks" such as doing an exercise or journal entry from this book or calling one person to set up an information interview.

Tool #6: Create your own job

Lists of job openings never include jobs that are waiting to be created. With a little imagination and analysis, you can create a job or career where none exists. Students have a long history of creating businesses to help pay the bills.

Some ideas are these:

- Typing papers and theses
- Computer consulting
- Babysitting and child care
- Gardening and lawn care
- Taking care of odd jobs and minor repairs
- Sewing and mending clothes
- Starting a delivery and errand service
- Painting and maintaining houses
- Taking photographs or producing videos of weddings and parties
- Working as a singing messenger
- Providing recorded or live music for parties and weddings
- Freelance editing and proofreading

Using the same kind of creativity, you can create a lifelong career. All it takes is looking for an unmet need that can be turned into a new service.

Another option is to redesign a job you already have. Sometimes existing companies allow employees to create jobs or businesses "within" a business. They may also allow for job sharing, converting a full-time job to a contract position, or working at home.

Tool #7: Attend to the details

The whole process of finding work may hang on details such as getting to appointments on time, respecting an interviewer's schedule, and staying no longer than agreed. Thanking people for their time, dressing appropriately for an interview, and sending follow-up notes can also be crucial.

To make your job search more effective, pay attention to these details. Ask yourself: What is one more thing I can do to make my job research complete or my presentation more effective?

EXERCISE

Translate goals into action

Choose one goal from your career plan. List that goal here:

_____

_____

Next, list some actions consistent with this goal. Ask yourself: What specific actions are needed to meet my goal? List those actions.

_____

Finally, translate any action you just listed into steps you could complete in less than one hour or start in the next 24 hours.

_____

_____

_____

You can apply this technique to any goal for your career or life. The point is to move ideas to action.

E X E R C I S E

Rehearse your job search

Suppose you completed your education today and your next task is to find a job in a field of interest to you. Imagine what it will be like to seek that job. The following questions will help you rehearse this job hunt. If you are unsure of your answers, write down your best guesses. Use separate paper as needed. The process of considering the question is much more valuable than any particular answer.

1. Where would you go to find work? Would you go to an existing company or try self-employment?

    _____
    _____
    _____

2. What job would you apply for? If you choose self-employment, what product or service would you offer?

    _____
    _____
    _____

3. Whom would you talk with about her job? Who is in charge of hiring? Can you talk with anyone at this firm before your job interview?

    _____
    _____
    _____

4. What specifically do you want to learn from your interview?

    _____
    _____
    _____

5. How likely is it that your first job will be your "dream" job? How long will it take you to reach your goal?

    _____
    _____
    _____

6. What kind of background, training, or experience do employers look for in people entering this field? What value do they place on formal education, training, and related experience?

    _____
    _____
    _____

Now review your responses. Do any of them suggest changes to make in your current course work or major? On separate paper, describe those changes.

Name ______________________ Date ____/____/____

JOURNAL ENTRY

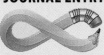

Discovery/Intention Statement

Think about approaches you've used to find jobs in the past. What did you do that worked in each of these cases?

What could you have done differently?

What did you learn from these experiences that could help your job searches in the future?

EXERCISE

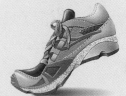

Create a support team

To fuel your energy for career planning, create your own support team. Begin by listing the names of three people with whom you will share your frustrations and successes in career planning and job hunting. These can be friends, family members, or classmates. Then ask these people to be on your team. Tell each team member your goals and intended actions. Ask them to help in holding you accountable to your plan. Touch base with each member of your team, either in person or by telephone, at least once each month.

List three candidates for your team. After you finalize the list, post a copy in a conspicuous place and use it. List each person's name, telephone number, and email address.

Tell everyone you know–the art of networking

Networking means developing and maintaining relationships with others. This means staying in touch with people to keep track of new ideas, services, or job openings.

Networking is most effective when done with persistence over a period of time. When it works, networking leads you effortlessly from one contact to another.

It's possible that jobs are filled more through networking than through any other method. Following are five ideas that can help you create and sustain your network.

Start with the people you already know

Brainstorm with your family and friends. Come up with a list of names—people who could help you with career planning or job hunting. Write each of these names on a 3x5 card or Rolodex card. You can also use a spiral-bound notebook or a computer. When you speak with someone on your list, make brief notes about what you discussed. Also jot down any further actions you promised to take.

Set up a job-hunting team

Stalking a job does not have to be a solitary affair. As an alternative, form a job-hunting group with others interested in your field. Working with other team members, you can share tasks, boosting your productivity with little or no extra effort.

For example, team members can help each other draft and revise résumés. They can alert each other to job openings and pair up to do information interviews. They can share notes from seminars, conventions, and workshops.

With the people in your group, you can share tears, dead ends, opportunities, laughter, sorrows, triumphs, bowling, and pizza. These people can be an important source of emotional support. Often the friendships formed in such groups last for many years—well beyond the time when everyone lands jobs.

Be open to making contacts

Consider everyone you meet a potential friend—and a valuable networking partner. Look for things you have in common. Students are often interested in hearing what others plan to do after graduating.

Develop a short statement of your career goal that you can easily share with people. For example: "After I graduate, I plan to work in the travel business. I'm looking for an internship in an established travel agency for next summer. Do you know of any that take interns?"

Get past the fear of competition

Networking intimidates some people. They fear that others will steal, hoard, or conceal job opportunities. "Why should I share this information with anybody?" goes the objection. "After all, we're competing with each other for the same jobs."

There are at least two answers to this question.

First, few people in any one network are actually competing for the same jobs. People majoring in broadcasting, for example, can have many career goals. Some want to be radio announcers. Others will look for work as videotape editors. Still others want to write television scripts or newscasts. Even people interested in the same jobs may be looking for positions with contrasting duties or in different parts of the country.

Second, any "competitor" could turn into a friend. Suppose someone in your network lands a job before you. This presents an opportunity. Send a note of congratulations to this person along with your address and phone number. This person may soon be in a position to recommend you for another opening—or even to hire you.

Follow up

Networking will uncover leads for you. These may be a person to call, a newsletter to read, or a definite job opening to pursue. Keeping these opportunities alive takes action. Often all that's needed is a follow-up letter, a résumé, some quick research, or a five-minute phone call. Any of these actions could bring your name before someone who can hire you.

Visit Houghton Mifflin's Career Planning web site for more ideas on how to make your network stronger: http://collegesurvival.college.hmco.com/students.

Revitalize your résumé

Your résumé is a living document that distills an essential part of your overall life plan. The attention you give to a résumé can pay you back hundreds of times over. Use a résumé to find a job that you love and land a salary that matches your talents.

Writing an effective résumé creates value in many ways. For one, a résumé can help you discover and express your skills by writing them down. It can serve as a calling card for you to leave with employers. It can remind you of key points you'd like to make in an interview. And a résumé can refresh a potential employer's memory after your interview. If you're applying for a job that's miles away from home, a résumé is essential.

A résumé is a piece of persuasive writing, not a laundry list of previous jobs or a dry recitation of facts. It has a basic purpose—to get you to the next step in the hiring process, usually an interview.

What follows are suggestions for résumés that get attention.

Avoid getting weeded out

Your résumé could be the most important document that you ever write. Yet most résumés fail. They get tossed, set aside, lost, or otherwise shuffled into oblivion. One goal in résumé writing is to get past the first cut.

Several things help achieve this goal. For example, neatness, organization, and correct grammar and punctuation are essential. Also, leave out any statements that could send your résumé hurtling into the circular file. Some items to delete or question are these:

- Boilerplate language—stock wording from standard job descriptions or commercial résumé services. Smart employers can sniff out such verbal fluff before they look at the mail.

- The date you're available to start a new job

- Salary information, including what you've made in the past and what you want to earn now

- Details about jobs you held more than 10 years ago

- Your reasons for leaving previous jobs

- Personal data, such as your religion, marital status, age, or weight. Employers can's legally ask about such items, and including them might hurt your prospects. Add personal data only if you're sure it can help you get the job.

Sometimes an offbeat approach will attract an employer's attention. One person applying for a job in public relations wrote his résumé as a press release meant to be read by a news announcer. A woman applying for work in an art museum designed her résumé as a collage. Before you use such a gimmick, carefully consider whether it will work with your potential employer.

Make it easy to skim

Knowing that employers devote little time to any individual résumé, you can design yours accordingly.

Begin with your name, address, and phone number. Then name your desired position, often called an "objective" or "goal." Follow with the body of your résumé—your abilities, achievements, experience, and education.

Write your résumé so that the key facts leap from the page. Leave "white space"—that is, avoid filling the page with ink. Describe your experience in short phrases and short paragraphs that start with action verbs: "Supervised one other person." "Set up sales calls." "Wrote two annual reports." Finally, organize your points under major headings, such as "Skills," "Education," and "Accomplishments." Putting those headings in bold print or in the left margin can make your résumé easy to skim.

Ask for feedback

To create a résumé that works, get feedback. Ask friends and family members if your résumé is easy to read and understand. Then adopt a practice used by most great writers—revise, revise, and revise some more. Create sparkling, polished paragraphs that demand a response.

Sell your skills as solutions

Every organization has problems to solve. Factories grapple with employee turnover. Software developers struggle to get their products out faster than the competition. Publishers seek ways to make their books

Keys to scannable résumés

Many companies use a computerized scanning program to catalog résumés and fill positions by using keyword searches. Human resources associates can quickly retrieve and route résumés to fill positions by matching their specifications with your qualifications. Including the right keywords on your résumé will help you stand out from others. Review job postings to find buzzwords that employers are searching for in your field of interest to include on your résumé. Get recognized by including specific positions and leadership roles you have held, related work experience, and degrees or certifications you have completed. Remember to also include your skills and core competencies.

Your scannable résumé should always be printed on one side of an 8½ x11 sheet of plain, white paper with an easy-to-read font and layout. If your résumé is more than one page in length, be sure your name and contact information appears on both sheets of paper. Avoid using italics, boldface, or underlining and other special text formatting. Do not staple or fold the résumé— it is best when hand-delivered or sent in an oversized envelope.

leap off the shelf and into buyers' hands. Your research can uncover the typical problems in your field—and even the specific problems your potential employer faces.

Show in your résumé that you know about these problems and can offer your skills as solutions. Whenever you can, give evidence that you used these skills to solve problems. For example, the skill you list might be "trained people to use word-processing software." If possible, talk about a time when you used that skill and describe the results: "Our program reduced the average training time by 25 percent."

As you write a résumé, give a fair shake to all your skills. Be sure to include content skills—any specialized knowledge or abilities you have. Also talk about transferable skills that apply across jobs.

Finish on a strong note

Most résumés just peter out at the end. As an alternative, include an intriguing statement ("I enjoy turning around departments with low morale") or even a favorable quote from one of your former supervisors ("Julio exceeded the requirements of his job in almost every case"). Use the last sentence to again sell your skills and solutions.

Combine your résumé with other strategies

Many people view résumés as the core of a job search. If you look at the ways résumés are actually used, you'll see evidence against this view. Employers who screen résumés may spend little time reading each one. They could have a stack of 30, 50, or even 100 résumés for a single job opening. Each résumé might get 30 seconds of attention or less. These figures have nothing to do with your skills, only with the constant pressures on human resources departments.

To get the most bang from your résumé, combine it with other job-hunting strategies. Research companies and do information interviews. Go ahead and contact employers directly, whether or not they have a job opening at the moment. Chat briefly with people who have the power to hire you; then leave your résumé with them. If you just send résumés and sit pining for a reply, you'll be disappointed.

When you do send a résumé, follow up. Call within two days after you think the employer will have received it. At that time, ask for an interview.

Also remember the full range of ways to remind an employer of your existence. You can send journal articles, news clippings, workshop announcements, thank-you notes, and follow-up letters. Send mail, faxes, or email. Add notes: "These are some items I think will interest you." Or "This is something you can file along with my résumé." If the company doesn't have a file on you yet, chances are someone will start one.

Sample résumés

The following résumés apply some of the ideas mentioned in this chapter. These examples are merely suggestions—not "right" ways to create a résumé. Read them only to spur your original thinking.

For more examples of résumés, visit Houghton Mifflin's Career Planning web site: **http://collegesurvival.college. hmco.com/students.**

LAMONT JACKSON

2250 First Avenue, #3 • New York, NY 10029 • (212) 222-5555
Lamont_Jackson44@hotmail.com

Objective

To obtain a position as a public relations associate that allows me to utilize my writing and communication skills.

Education

Rutgers University, New Brunswick, NJ
BA in English, Minor in Business Communication; May 2001
Major GPA—3.2; Minor GPA—3.3

Experience

The Medium, Rutgers University, New Brunswick, NJ
Contributing Writer, August 1999–May 2001
- Developed feature articles pertaining to faculty and student issues on campus and community issues.
- Responsible for writing weekly sidebar featuring community service on and off campus.

Shandwick Public Relations, New York, NY
Intern, Summer 2000
- Coordinated mass mailings of press releases to medical community biweekly.
- Conducted health surveys focusing on nutrition habits of senior citizens in the tristate area; organized all retrieved data of 1000 respondents.
- Handled telephone inquiries from clients and corporations represented by firm.

Activities

- Men's Intramural Soccer Team, Spring 2001
- Habitat for Humanity, *Treasurer,* Fall 1999–Spring 2000
- Rutgers University Orientation Leader, Summer 1999

Skills

- Ability to perform on both PC and Macintosh platforms.
- Software knowledge that includes Windows NT, Microsoft Office, Lotus Notes, Lotus 1-2-3, Quark, and beginner HTML.
- Fluency in Spanish—oral and written competency.

Honors

- Rutgers University Dean's List, Fall 1999, Spring 2001

Susan Chang
2500 North Highland Avenue · Atlanta, GA 30306
770-899-8707
susangeorgia276@aol.com

Work Experience:	**LAND Enterprises, Inc., Atlanta, GA**
	Administrative Assistant January 2002—present
	· Responsible for supporting national sales
	  manager and three district managers in creating
	  reports for nationwide sales staff.
	· Create, prepare, and maintain Excel spreadsheets
	  with weekly sales data.
	· Manage sales representative calendar of events
	  in Lotus Notes database.
	
	Peachtree Bank, Alpharetta, GA
	Teller May 2001—December 2001
	· Was responsible for receiving cash/checks for
	  deposits, processed withdrawals, and accepted
	  loan payments.
	· Communicated with customers and provided account
	  balance and savings and loan information.
	· Provided friendly and prompt customer service.

Education:	**Macon State College, Macon, GA** BS—Communications and Information Technology; May 2001 Overall GPA: 3.0

Volunteer:	**Macon Chamber of Commerce**
	Holiday Events Coordinator 2000—2001
	· Maintained budget from Chamber of Commerce for
	  annual holiday parties.
	· Solicited donations from local businesses to
	  support monthly events.

Computer Skills:	Microsoft Word, Microsoft Excel, Microsoft Access, Lotus Notes, PowerPoint.
Personal:	Interested in writing poetry, playing team sports, and traveling.
References:	Available upon request.

Scannable résumé

Marco Juarez
1200 South Michigan Avenue
Chicago, IL 60605
312-343-0317
juarezm17@yahoo.com

Job Objective: Training Manager

Work Experience: Trainer, Omega Software, Chicago, IL
1993–present

ACHIEVEMENTS AS MANAGER OF HUMAN RESOURCES
-Developed the Training Audit—a new method of evaluating
the efficiency and effectiveness of corporate training programs.
-Trained managers from 20 companies to use the Training Audit.
-Conducted 230 performance reviews.
-Designed and implemented training programs.
-Developed and presented courses in basic business writing,
mathematics, listening, reading, and conflict resolution.
-Established training department for software.
-Presented courses on customer service to 500 participants.
-Translated core training materials from English to Spanish.
-Revised job descriptions and procedures manuals.

ACHIEVEMENTS IN COMMUNICATING
WITH WIDER AUDIENCES
-Designed and presented seminars: "Conflict Resolution Across
Cultures," "Managing a Diverse Workforce: 10 Strategies That
Make a Difference," and "Managing Workers Who
Telecommute."
-Wrote 12 articles for industry publications about multicultural
perspectives on conflict resolution.
-Spoke to 45 community groups about issues faced by Hispanic
workers in the United States.

Education: Columbia College Chicago
BS Technical Communications; May 1993.
Dean's List: Fall 1992, Spring 1992.

References: Available upon request.

Sell your résumé with an effective cover letter

An effective cover letter can leave a prospective employer waiting with bated breath to read your résumé. An ineffective letter can propel your résumé to that nefarious stack of papers to be read "later." In some cases, a well-written letter alone can land you an interview.

Many cover letters are little more than a list of stock phrases. Reduced to their essence, they say, "I want that job you listed. Here's my résumé. Read it."

You can write a more interesting letter that practically demands action. Using a three-part structure can help you accomplish this goal.

1 In your first sentence, grab the employer's attention. Make a statement that appeals directly to the employer's self-interest. Mention a persistent problem that the employer faces. Then offer your skills and knowledge as a solution. Write something that moves the employer to say, "We can't afford to pass this person up. Call her right away to set up an appointment."

2 Second, build interest. Add some facts to back up your opening paragraph. Briefly refer to your past experience and highlight one or two key achievements. If you're applying for a specific job opening, say so. If you have no specific position in mind, offer an idea that will intrigue the employer enough to respond anyway.

3 Finally, take care of business. Refer the reader to your résumé. Then mention that you'll call at a specific time to set up an interview.

Keep your letter short—two or three paragraphs. Employers are busy people. Reading cover letters is probably not high on their list of fun things to do. Keeping your letter short is also a timesaver for you.

Correspondence Quick Tips

Use these additional suggestions for making your cover letter a must read.

- Address your letter to a specific individual. Make sure to use the correct title and mailing address.
- Use a simple typeface that is easy to read.
- Tailor each letter you write to the specific company and position you are applying for.
- Be honest. An employer may choose to ask you questions about information you present in your cover letter during an interview. Be prepared to expand upon and support your statements.
- Thank your reader for their time and consideration.
- Check for typographical, grammatical and word usage errors. Do not rely on your computer to spell check.
- Ask someone to read over your letter before you send it out. An extra pair of eyes may help you uncover errors.
- Use high quality paper stock for your hard copy letters.
- When sending cover letters via email, use a meaningful subject header and a professional tone (do not use emoticons :-)). Be sure to include your phone number in case the contact prefers to follow up with you via phone.
- When faxing a cover letter and résumé, indicate the total number pages in the transmission.

Sample cover letters

The following are the main paragraphs of sample cover letters. Comb them for ideas that you like. These examples are simply suggestions, not prescriptions for the "right" ways to write a cover letter.

Remember to personalize your cover letters. Address each letter to an individual—the person who can hire you. Also include your name, address, phone number, email address, and signature.

Example #1
Written by a person seeking a position in the auto industry.

> Please allow me to introduce myself. My name is Ralph Moore and I recently moved to this area. I have worked in the auto industry for the past 17 years, and I am interested in continuing in that industry as a worker for DWC Radiators. I worked for Angelo's Auto Supplies in Lansing, Michigan, before moving to Minnesota.
>
> My background is in the repairs department. I played a key role on the team that serviced imported radiators. I have excellent references from my former employer.
>
> I will stop by your office next Wednesday afternoon to fill out a formal application. If you could take a few minutes to see me at that time, I would be very grateful. I will give you a call on Tuesday to see if this can be arranged.

Example #2
Written by a recent graduate seeking a job as an editorial assistant at a magazine.

> As a recent college graduate, I am the perfect candidate for your entry-level position as an editorial assistant for Seventeen magazine. During my studies, I have held three positions at my college's magazine, including Features Editor, Campus Correspondent, and Senior Copyeditor. In my senior year, I initiated a new section in our magazine, Style File, featuring local clothing and accessories stores. Featuring a similar Style File in your magazine from different cities across the nation would be an intriguing section for your readers.
>
> I am proficient in using both PC and MAC platforms and have skills using programs in the Microsoft Office Suite and Quark. The enclosed résumé explains how my past positions and other qualifications are a perfect fit for your opening. I will call you in a few days to schedule a time when we can talk in more detail.

Example #3

Written in response to a job posting for a program coordinator.

> The flyer announcing the position of Program Coordinator caught my attention immediately. This position interests me because I have the skills required to work on a diverse team. I am fluent in Spanish, French, and English and have had a longstanding interest in working with people from many cultures. My experience as a vendor in an Argentina zoo and my current job as unit manager at the UN Communications Center are two examples of the unique and relevant background I would bring to the position of Program Coordinator at the UC International House.
>
> As a member of the International House, I also have a firsthand understanding about how residents feel about the activities and special events hosted by this office throughout the year. Because of this, I am in an excellent position to help plan a variety of activities residents will appreciate.
>
> As directed in the job announcement, I am requesting an appointment for an interview on March 28, between 2 p.m. and 6 p.m., at a time convenient for you. Please contact me if another time is more appropriate. Thank you very much for your time and consideration.

Example #4

Written by a person who is seeking a job and learned about a possible opening through networking.

> Your Chief Financial Officer, Elena Perez, told me recently that you were looking for an MIS director. Because of my background, she encouraged me to contact you directly. I am very impressed with the growth your company made in the past two years. With that kind of expansion, I can understand your need to create a separate MIS department.
>
> This position relates well to my current experience at Murphy and Sons, LLP as you will see from my enclosed résumé. I possess a diversified background that would enable me to serve your organization's MIS needs efficiently. I am a creative and highly motivated individual with good communication and interpersonal skills. I am confident that these qualifications coupled with my work ethic and enthusiasm would allow me to make a positive contribution to your company.
>
> I welcome the opportunity to meet with you to discuss how my qualifications may best meet your needs. Thank you in advance for your time and consideration.

When posting your résumé online, include a cover memo, such as the example here, with key information from your résumé and a detailed explanation of your objective.

> Subject: Seeking advertising account position
>
> I am interested in finding a position with a major advertising firm. I have worked in advertising for four years. As a junior advertising assistant, my duties include contract negotiation, lead liaison, and creative development. My present account assignments include Intel, Cisco, Coca-Cola, and Ford.
>
> My attached résumé includes information about my work history, including related internship experiences in advertising. Please email me at mraj212@mindspring.com.
>
> Attached: MRAJ Resume.doc

Use interviews to hire yourself an employer

The young man's palms are sweating, his heart pounding. He notices his hands are shaking; it's hard to button his coat. He fumbles for his keys. Locking the door, he hopes he'll return that night with good news. Huddled against the cold, he slouches out the door, eyes cast downward, walking with short, clipped steps. He's got to hurry. Being late for this appointment could dash his already meager chances.

This is the way many people experience the last moments before a job interview. Instead of sensing opportunity, they feel as if they're about to be sentenced for a crime.

Job interviews don't have to work this way. In fact, they can be exhilarating. They offer a way to meet people. They give you a chance to present your skills. They can expand your network of contacts.

An interview is a chance for you to assess a job and work environment. You're out to see if this position is something you really want. By interviewing, you're "hiring" an employer.

Many of the ideas that apply to writing résumés also apply to preparing for an interview. Learn everything you can about the company. Know your skills, and talk about how your skills can benefit the employer. Other ways to get the most out of an interview include the following.

Anticipate questions and rehearse answers

Skilled interviewers have many questions. Most of them boil down to a few major concerns:

- Would we be comfortable working with you?
- How did you find out about us?
- How can you help us?
- Will you learn this job quickly?
- What makes you different from other applicants?
- Will you work for a salary we can afford?

Before your interview, prepare some answers to these questions. Explain how your research led you to the company. Focus on solving the employer's problems and talk about skills or experiences that make you stand out from the crowd. Speak briefly and directly to the point.

To make your job interviews more effective, look for chances to practice. Information interviews are one way to do this. Role-playing can also work well. Enroll a friend to play the part of the interviewer and ask you the six questions or variations of them. When you're done, ask your friend for feedback.

Also be alert to any inconsistencies in your answers. For example, if you say that you're a "team player" but prefer to work independently, be prepared to explain.

Start on a positive note and stay there

Many interviewers make their decision about an applicant early on. In one study, interviewers were videotaped as they talked with job applicants. These interviewers were asked to snap their fingers when they'd made a decision about hiring the applicant. Most snapped their fingers within the first five minutes of the interview.

With this in mind, start on a positive note. Work to make things go well in the first few minutes of the interview. Even if you're nervous, you can be outgoing and attentive.

One way to create a favorable first impression is through the way you look. Be well groomed. Wear clothing that's appropriate for the employer's work environment.

Also, monitor your nonverbal language. Give a firm handshake and make eye contact (without looking like a zombie). Sit in a way that says you're at ease with people and have a high energy level. During the interview, seize opportunities to smile or even tell an amusing story, as long as it's relevant and positive.

As the interview gets rolling, search for common ground. Finding out that you share an interest with an interviewer can make the conversation sail—and put you closer to a job offer. You can demonstrate interest through focused attention. Listen carefully to everything interviewers say. Few of them will mind if you take notes, and this might even impress them.

As the interviewer speaks, listen for challenges that the company faces. Then paint yourself as a problem solver. Explain how you've met similar challenges in the past and what you can do for the employer right now. To support your claims, mention a detail or two about your accomplishments and refer the interviewer to your résumé for more.

Once you hit a positive note, do everything possible to stay there. For example, when speaking about others, be courteous. If you find it hard to say something positive about a coworker or employer, shift the focus back to the employer's needs.

As the interview proceeds, show that you know the value of time. If your appointment time is scheduled to end soon, mention this to the interviewer. Give that person the option to end the conversation or to extend the interview time.

Ask open-ended questions and listen

Come with your own list of questions for the employer. Skilled interviewers will usually leave time for you to ask these.

Through your questions, aim at finding out the following facts:

- What qualifications the job requires—and whether your preferred skills and experience are a match
- Whether the job meshes with your values and your preferences for a working environment
- Whether the job involves contact with people you'd enjoy
- Whether you can get the salary you want

After you ask a question, give the interviewer plenty of time to talk. One guideline is to listen at least 50 percent of the time.

Keep the key facts at your command

Remembering essential information during an interview can help things go smoothly. To jog your memory, keep certain information handy. Examples are a list of references, your social security number, and a summary of your work history. To this add the main points you'd like to get across in the interview. You can type this information on a sheet of paper that fits in a folder or portfolio. Consider making several copies of this document and leaving it with the person who interviews you.

When appropriate, take the initiative

Keep in mind that the person you're talking with might be uncomfortable with interviewing. Many people have little training in this area. They might dominate the conversation, interrupt you, or go blank and forget what they want to ask.

When things like this happen, you can take the initiative. Ask for time to get your questions answered. Sum up your key qualifications, and request a detailed job description.

Some companies use structured interviews. Here, a group of people meet with each job candidate and ask similar questions each time. The idea behind this technique is to make sure everyone who applies is treated fairly and has an equal chance of getting hired.

Used ineffectively, structured interviews can be artificial or limiting. If you feel this way, remember the key points you want to make about yourself. Look for every opportunity to weave these points into your answers.

Choose your conversation

Many interviews naturally come to rest in the past—your prior education and work history. Experiment with steering the conversation toward the future. Emphasize what you can accomplish for the employer in the next quarter, year, five years, or decade. Talk about the fit between your goals and the employer's goals. Doing so can raise the pitch of the conversation and spark an employer's interest.

Give yourself a raise before you start work

Effective salary discussion can make a huge difference to your financial well-being. Consider the potential impact of making just an extra $1000 per year. That's an extra $5000 in your pocket after five years, even assuming you get no other raises.

It's possible to discuss salary too early. Rather than bringing it up, let the interviewer take the initiative.

One ideal time to talk about salary is when an employer is ready to offer you a job—and when you're interested in accepting. At this point the employer might be willing to part with more money.

Employers often use a standard negotiating strategy. First, they come to the interview with a salary range in mind. Then they offer a starting salary at the lower end of that range.

This strategy holds an important message for you: Salaries are flexible, especially for higher-level jobs. You don't usually have to accept the first salary offer.

When you finally get down to money, be prepared. Begin by knowing the salary range that you prefer. First, figure out how much money you need to sustain your desired standard of living. Then add some margin for comfort. If you're in doubt, add 10 percent to your current salary and consider asking for that amount. Add in the value of any benefits the employer provides.

Sometimes you can look up standard pay ranges for certain jobs. Reference books such as the *Occupational Outlook Handbook* include this information. (Ask a librarian for help.) Also ask friends or acquaintances who work in your field, and review your notes from information interviews. Another option is the obvious one—ask interviewers what salary range they have in mind.

Once you're confident you know that range, aim high. Name some figures toward the upper end and see how the interviewer responds. Starting high gives you some room to negotiate. Also state a desired range at first, rather than a fixed figure. See if you can win a raise now rather than later.

Use each "No" to come one step closer to "Yes"

Almost everyone who's ever applied for a job knows the refrains: "We have no openings for you right now." "We'll keep your résumé on file." "There were many qualified applicants for this job." "Even though you were not chosen, we thank you for applying." "Best of luck as you pursue other career opportunities."

Each of those is a different way of saying no. And they can hurt.

Yet *no* does not have to be the final word. Focus on the future. If you're turned down for a job, consider what could turn that *no* into a *yes* next time you interview. Could you fine-tune your résumé? Could you present yourself differently during the interview? Could you do more thorough research? Can you fine-tune your goals? You can even pose these questions to the person who interviewed you. Also ask for referrals to people in your field, either inside or outside the company.

Consider what a job rejection really means. When an employer says no, this is not an eternal judgment of your character. It reflects only what happened between you and one potential employer, often in a few hours or just a few minutes. It means no for right now, for this job, for today—not for every job, forever.

Eventually an employer or client will hire you. It is just a matter of time before the inevitable *yes*. When you're turned down for a job, this is just one more *no* that's out of the way.

Follow up

Within 24 hours, send a thank-you note to the person who interviewed you. To personalize your note, mention a relevant detail from your conversation. Prompt follow-up can make you stand out in an interviewer's mind. Also send thank-you's to anyone else who helped you get the interview—receptionists, assistants, or contacts within the company.

 For sample interview questions to ask future employers and sample questions to practice answering, visit Houghton Mifflin's Career Planning web site: **http://collegesurvival. college.hmco.com/students.**

Sample thank-you notes

A thank-you note can be as important as the interview itself—especially if an employer uses your letter as a deciding factor. Include information in your note that will help remind the employer of your conversation, and follow up with any further thoughts you may have had after your interview.

I wanted to take the time to thank you for meeting with me yesterday. Learning about the day-to-day aspects of magazine publishing at Time, Inc. has increased my level of interest in the position of Editorial Assistant at your company. Your team shares my level of motivation and interest in writing creative copy and unique products in magazine development. Thank you for inviting the Managing Editor and his Editorial Assistant to speak with me, too. It was helpful to hear about the position from their perspectives.

I am enclosing my references as per your request. I look forward to hearing from you soon.

Thank you for taking the time to meet with me on Monday. I enjoyed learning about BabyMint.com and the role of the IT group.

As I mentioned in the interview, I would be very interested in the Siebel Business Analyst position and feel that I could be an asset to BabyMint.com. Thank you for your consideration. I look forward to hearing from you soon.

I enjoyed my interview with you and Ms. Edmonds last Thursday, and I want to thank you for taking the time to show me around your facilities and providing information about Global Enterprises, Inc. My experiences at Southwest Communications as Marketing Associate have prepared me for the role of Marketing Director at your company. I reviewed the internal web site that you provided me access to; I was impressed with the development that was done to keep your employees informed of company information.

If you have any questions about my resume, please call me at (212) 555-1234, or email me at mjstevens@nynet.com.

1 Describe three strategies for finding work that are likely to increase your chances of getting the job you want.

2 Briefly describe the process of networking and its benefits.

3 List three strategies for writing résumés that get attention.

4 How will you make sure your cover letter will catch the attention of the employer you are writing to?

5 What actions should you take to prepare for an interview?

One must learn by doing the thing, for though you think you know it, you have no certainty until you try.
ARISTOTLE

The most important single ingredient in the formula of success is knowing how to get along with people.
THEODORE ROOSEVELT

IN THIS CHAPTER ... Find success in working with your coworkers by learning about their preferences and styles. Join a diverse workplace. Forget your career—lift your eyes from the details of career planning to the larger horizon. Create your life purpose, review your core values, and think about long-range goals. Celebrate your plan—then begin again.

Succeeding with coworkers– it's a matter of style

Imagine finding the "perfect" job, showing up for your first day of work—and then wanting to quit after just one week with your coworkers.

First there's the man across the hall from you. He never sits still. During meetings, he likes to pace around the room. Whenever you have a new idea, he wants to discuss it while taking a walk.

Then there's the guy in the next cubicle. He works in sales, and he's always talking. He spends five hours a day on the phone talking to customers. He spends another two hours talking to coworkers. On top of that, he talks to himself whenever he's trying to solve a problem.

And there's your supervisor. She hardly talks at all. You never hear her phone ring. She relies on email to communicate with you—even though her office is 20 feet away from yours. She also wants requests, plans, and key actions documented in writing.

You might wonder how all these people can stand each other, let alone get anything done. Perhaps you pictured the ideal office as a place where people create a common culture and meet their quarterly goals with the precision of a synchronized swimming team. Instead, you're stuck with a group of people from different planets.

Recognize styles as preferences

Your coworkers aren't trying to irritate you. Their behaviors simply express a variety of preferences for perceiving information, processing ideas, and acting on what they learn.

The man who's continually moving prefers concrete experience over memos and meetings. He likes to learn by doing.

The man who's continually on the phone prefers to learn by listening and talking. He likes to reflect on his experience and forge relationships.

In contrast, your supervisor enjoys working with concepts as much as working with people. She wants a long-range vision and a detailed plan before she moves into action.

Discover styles in your workplace

You can learn a lot about your coworkers' styles simply by observing them during the workday. Just look for clues.

One clue is their *approaches to a learning task*. Some people process new information ideas by sitting quietly and reading or writing. When learning to use a piece of equipment, such as a new computer, they'll read the instruction manual first. Others will skip the manual, unpack all the boxes and start setting up equipment. And other coworkers might ask a more experienced colleague to guide them in person, step by step.

Another clue is *word choice*. Some people like to process information visually. You might hear them say, "I'll look into that" or "Give me the big picture first." Others like to solve problems verbally: "Let's talk through this problem" or "I hear you!" In contrast, some of your coworkers focus on body sensations ("This product feels great") or action ("Let's run with this idea and see what happens").

You can also observe *body language*. Notice how often coworkers make eye contact with you and how close they sit or stand next to you. Observe their gestures as well as the volume and tone of their voice.

Your coworkers will display a variety of other preferences. Notice *content preferences*—that is, which subjects they openly discuss at work and which topics they avoid. Some people talk freely about their feelings, their families, and even their personal finances. Others choose to remain silent on such topics and stick to work-related matters.

In addition, notice *process preferences*—patterns in the way that your coworkers meet goals. When attending meetings, for example, some might stick closely to the agenda and keep an eye on the clock. Other people might prefer to "go with the flow" even if it means working an extra hour or scrapping the agenda.

Once you've discovered such differences among your coworkers, look for ways to accommodate their styles. This is a key idea to remember when making presentations, planning projects, and resolving conflict.

Gear presentations to different styles

When you want coworkers to agree to a new procedure or promote a new product, you'll probably make a speech or give a presentation. To persuade more people, gear your presentation to several styles.

For people who want to see the big picture first, you can start by saying, "This product has four major features." Then explain the benefits of each feature in order.

Also allow time for people to ask questions and make comments. Offer them a chance to try out the new product for themselves—to literally "get the feel of it."

Finish with a handout that includes plenty of visuals and step-by-step instructions. Visual learners and people who like to think abstractly will appreciate it.

Gear projects to different styles

An understanding of styles can also make or break your next major project at work. When designing a project, an effective manager makes time for each major aspect of the learning cycle:

- *Planning*—defining the desired outcomes, assigning major tasks, setting due dates for each task, and generating commitment to action
- *Doing*—carrying out assigned tasks
- *Reflecting*—meeting regularly to discuss what's working well and ways to improve the next phase of the project
- *Interpreting*—discussing what the team has learned from the project and ways to apply that learning to the whole organization

When working on project teams, look for ways to combine skills in complementary ways. If you're skilled at planning, find someone who excels at doing. Also seek people who can reflect on and interpret the team's experience. Pooling different styles allows you to draw on everyone's strengths.

Resolve conflict with respect for styles

When people's styles clash in the workplace, we have several options. One is to throw up our hands and resign ourselves to personality conflicts. Another option is to recognize differences, accept them, and respect them as complementary ways to meet common goals.

To begin, see if you can resolve any conflict within yourself. You might have mental pictures about workplaces as places where people are all "supposed" to have the same style. Notice those pictures and gently let them go. If you expect differences in styles, you can more easily respect those differences.

In many cases, you can resolve conflicts simply by letting people take on the kinds of tasks that fit their learning style. As you do, remember that style is both stable and dynamic. People gravitate toward the kinds of tasks they've succeeded at in the past. They can also broaden their styles by taking on new tasks to reinforce different aspects of learning. For example, people who enjoy taking immediate action can learn to step back more often and reflect on the overall purpose of a project.

See the workplace as a learning place

Succeeding with coworkers means seeing the workplace as a laboratory for learning from experience. In this laboratory, we get to immerse ourselves in action and accomplish tasks. We also get to reflect continually on our experience, discover key insights, and create powerful intentions. Resolving conflict and learning from mistakes are all part of the learning cycle.

As the workplace becomes more diverse and technology creates a global marketplace, you'll work with people who differ from you in profound ways. Differences in style can be a stumbling block or an opportunity. When differences intersect, there is the potential for conflict—and for creativity.

 For more ideas on succeeding at work in the global marketplace, visit Houghton Mifflin's Career Planning web site: http://collegesurvival.college.hmco.com/students.

JOURNAL ENTRY

Discovery/Intention Statement

After reading the article *Succeeding with coworkers—it's a matter of style,* reflect for a moment on your own learning style. Describe your preferences for learning and for accomplishing tasks in the workplace. Include specific examples.

I discovered that I . . .

_____

_____

_____

_____

_____

_____

_____

_____

_____

_____

_____

_____

_____

Next, think of one conflict at school or work that could stem from a difference in styles. Brainstorm a list of possible solutions. Then choose one that you can put into action.

I intend to . . .

_____

_____

_____

_____

_____

_____

_____

_____

_____

_____

_____

_____

_____

Join a diverse workplace

Today our work force is multicultural. This trend will continue well into the future. The *Report on the American Workforce 2001* concluded that "[b]arring a return to the exclusionary immigration policies of the 1920's, the United States likely will continue to be a nation in which increasing racial and ethnic diversity is the rule, not the exception. As in the past, people of diverse backgrounds will continue to contribute to a common culture, while maintaining many elements of their own cultural identities that help link them to their origins." By 2008, the Department of Labor predicts that 27 percent of the total civilian work force will be either African American, Hispanic, or Asian. Your next boss or coworker could be a person whose life experience and view of the world differ radically from yours.

People of all races, ethnicities, and cultures can use the following strategies to reach common ground.

Expect differences

To prevent breakdowns in communication, remember an obvious fact: People differ. Simple as it is, this truth is easy to forget. Most of us unconsciously judge others by a single set of standards—our own. Consider some examples:

- A man in Costa Rica works for a multinational company. He turns down a promotion that would take his family to Minnesota. His colleagues are mystified by this choice. Yet the man has grandparents in ill health, and leaving them behind would be taboo in his country.

- A Native American woman avoids eye contact with her supervisors. Her coworkers see her as aloof. Actually, people in her culture seldom make eye contact with their superiors.

Try to speak simply and directly, and enunciate clearly. If you're in English-speaking countries, speak Standard English while at work. Using street language or slang can leave your listeners adrift.

Also remember that gestures differ in meaning. For example, people from India may shake their heads from side to side to indicate agreement—not disagreement. The hand signal that signifies "OK" in America (thumb and index finger forming a circle) is considered obscene in Brazil.

• A North American Caucasian travels to Brazil on business. She shows up promptly for a 9 a.m. meeting to discover that the meeting starts 30 minutes late and goes an hour behind its scheduled time. She's entered a culture with a more flexible sense of time than she is used to.

To prevent misunderstandings, remember that culture touches every aspect of life. Differences in culture could affect each encounter you have with another person. Expecting differences helps you keep an open mind and lays the groundwork for all of the remaining strategies.

Use language with care

Even people who speak the same language can use simple words to confuse each other. For example, giving someone a "mickey" can mean pulling a practical joke—or slipping a drug into someone's drink. We find it hard enough to communicate simple facts, let alone abstract concepts.

To prevent confusion, avoid ambiguous words. Also use synonyms with care. Even slight differences in word meaning can pollute your message.

Put messages in context

When speaking to people of another culture, you might find that the words carry only part of their intended message. In many countries, strong networks of shared beliefs and assumptions form a context for all communication. For example, people from some Asian and Arabic countries might not include every detail of an agreement in a written contract. These people often place a high value on keeping verbal promises. Spelling out all the details in writing might be considered an insult. Knowing such facts can help you prevent and resolve conflicts in the workplace.

Test for understanding

To promote cross-cultural understanding, look for signs that your message got through clearly. Ask questions without talking down to your audience: "Am I making myself clear?" "Is there anything you don't understand?" Watch for nonverbal cues of understanding such as a nod or smile.

Relate to individuals, not "cultures"

One powerful way to overcome stereotypes is to treat each person as an individual. When we see people as faceless representatives of a race or ethnic group, we gloss over important differences. A solution is to remember that members of any culture can vary widely in beliefs and behaviors.

Discover what you share

The word *communicate* is closely related to *commune* and *common*. This fact points to a useful strategy: When relating to people of another culture, search for what you have in common.

You can start on the job. People from different cultures can share many values related to working. Examples are the desire to make more money, be recognized for achievement, or win promotions. Cultures often overlap at the level of basic human values—desires for safety, health, and economic security.

Learn about another culture

You can promote cross-cultural understanding through the path of knowledge. Consider learning everything you can about another culture. Begin by reading or going to museums, lectures, and classes.

Follow up with action. When you're at work, join project teams with diverse members. Cultivate friends from another culture. Also take part in their community events. Get a feel for the customs, music, and art that members of a group share. If appropriate, travel to another country.

Learn about your company culture

Each company, large or small, develops its own culture—a set of shared values and basic assumptions. Even if you're self-employed, you can benefit by knowing your clients' corporate cultures.

Notice the unwritten codes of behavior in an organization. The next people you work with might live by "rules" such as these: Never make the boss look bad. . . . Make and keep commitments. . . . If you want to get promoted, be visible. . . . Everyone's expected to work some overtime.

One way to thrive in almost any corporate culture is to build a reputation for excellence. Take on tough assignments. Instead of complaining, make a request or propose a solution. Perform beyond requirements and give due credit to coworkers.

Expand networks

People with narrow circles of relationships can be at a disadvantage when trying to change jobs or enter a new field. For maximum flexibility in your career, affirm your culture—and cultivate contacts with people of other cultures.

Counter bias and discrimination

Title VII of the Civil Rights Act bans discrimination in virtually all aspects of working, from hiring and transfers to promotion and firing. Congress set up the Equal Employment Opportunity Commission (EEOC) to enforce this act.

If you think you've been the subject of discrimination, take time to examine the facts first. In cases of layoffs, look for other possible factors. Perhaps your company reorganized, completed a merger, lost a major contract, or went through a sales slump. Find out if other employees lost their jobs also.

While you're working, keep records of your performance. Log your achievements. Ask for copies of your performance evaluations and make sure they're accurate. If you ever go to court, having a stack of favorable evaluations can work in your favor.

Even under current law, you might find it hard to prove discrimination. Weigh the costs and benefits of any action you take. Before filing a lawsuit, exhaust other options. Start with your supervisor, your company's equal employment officer, or someone from the EEOC.

Be willing to bridge gaps

Being willing to bridge culture gaps might be more crucial than knowing another group's customs or learning a new language. Begin by being open-minded and willing to suspend judgment. People from other cultures could sense these qualities and reach out to you.

To communicate across cultures, beware of absolutes and ethnocentrism— "My culture, right or wrong." Becoming aware of your biases means thinking critically, listening fully, and even feeling uncomfortable at times.

It's worth it. You can enjoy new chances to learn, increase your career options, and expand your friendships. The ability to work with people of many cultures is a marketable skill—and a way to enlarge your world.

Dealing with sexism and sexual harassment

Sexism and sexual harassment are real. They are terms for events that occur at vocational schools, colleges, and universities throughout the world. Nearly all of these incidents are illegal or against school policies.

In the United States, women make up the majority of first-year students in higher education. Yet until the early nineteenth century, they were banned from colleges and universities. Today women in higher education still encounter bias based on gender.

This bias can take many forms. For example, instructors might gloss over the contributions of women. Students in philosophy class might never hear of a woman named Hypatia, an ancient Greek philosopher and mathematician. Those majoring in computer science might never learn about Grace Hopper, who developed a computer language named COBOL. And your art history textbook might not mention the Mexican painter Frida Kahlo or the American painter Georgia O'Keeffe.

Though men can be subjects of sexism and sexual harassment, women are more likely to experience this form of discrimination. Even the most well-intentioned people might behave in ways that hurt or discount women. Sexism takes place when:

- Instructors use only masculine pronouns—*he, his,* and *him*—to refer to both men and women.

- Career counselors hint that careers in mathematics and science are not appropriate for women.

- Students pay more attention to feedback from a male teacher than from a female teacher.

- Woman are not called on in class, their comments are ignored, or they are overly praised for answering the simplest questions.

- Examples given in a textbook or lecture assign women only to traditionally "female" roles—wife, mother, day care provider, elementary school teacher, nurse, and the like.

- People assume that middle-aged women who return to school have too many family commitments to study adequately or do well in their classes.

Many kinds of behavior—both verbal and physical—fall under the title of sexual harassment. This kind of discrimination involves unwelcome sexual conduct. The following are examples of such conduct in a school setting:

- Sexual touching or advances

- Any other unwanted touch

- Unwanted verbal intimacy

- Sexual graffiti

- Displaying or distributing sexually explicit materials

- Sexual gestures and jokes

- Pressure for sexual favors

- Talking about personal sexual activity

- Spreading rumors about someone's sexual activity or rating someone's sexual performance

Sexual Harassment: It's Not Academic, a pamphlet from the U.S. Department of Education, quotes a woman who experienced sexual harassment in higher education: "The financial officer made it clear that I could get the money I needed if I slept with him."

That's an example of *quid pro quo harassment.* This legal term applies when students believe that an educational decision depends on submitting to unwelcome sexual conduct. *Hostile environment harassment* takes place when such incidents are severe, persistent, or pervasive.

The feminist movement has raised our awareness about discrimination against women. We can now respond to sexism and sexual harassment in the places we live, work, and go to school. Specific strategies follow.

Point out sexist language and behavior

When you see examples of sexism, point them out. Your message can be more effective if you indicate the specific statements and behaviors that you consider sexist, instead of personal attacks.

For example, you could rephrase a sexist comment so that it targets another group, such as Jews or African Americans. People might spot anti-Semitism or racism more readily than sexism.

Keep in mind that men can also be subjected to sexism, ranging from antagonistic humor to exclusion from jobs that have traditionally been done by women.

Observe your own language and behavior

Looking for sexist behavior in others is effective. Detecting it in yourself can be just as powerful. Write a Discovery Statement about specific comments that could be interpreted as sexist. Then notice if you say any of these things. Also ask people you know to point out occasions when you use similar statements. Follow up with an Intention Statement that describes how you plan to change your speaking or behavior.

You can also write Discovery Statements about the current level of intimacy (physical and verbal) in any of your relationships at home, work, or school. Be sure that any increase in the level of intimacy is mutually agreed upon.

Encourage support for women

Through networks, women can work to overcome the effects of sexism. Strategies include study groups for women, women's job networks, and professional organizations, such as Women in Communications. Other examples are counseling services and health centers for women, family planning agencies, and rape prevention centers. Check your school catalog and library to see if any of these services are available at your school.

If your school does not have the women's networks you want, you can help form them. Sponsor a one-day or one-week conference on women's issues. Create a discussion or reading group for the women in your class, department, residence hall, union, or neighborhood.

Set limits

Women, value yourselves. Recognize your right to an education without the distraction of inappropriate and invasive behavior. Trust your judgment about when your privacy or your rights are being violated. Decide now what kind of sexual comments and actions you're uncomfortable with—and refuse to put up with them.

If you are sexually harassed, take action

Some key federal legislation protects the rights of women. One is Title VII of the Civil Rights Act of 1964. Guidelines for interpreting this law offer the following definition of harassment:

Unwelcome sexual advances, requests for sexual favors, and other verbal or physical conduct of a sexual nature constitute sexual harassment when:

1 *Submission to this conduct becomes a condition of employment.*

2 *Women's response to such conduct is used as a basis for employment decisions.*

3 *This conduct interferes with work performance or creates an offensive work environment.*

The law also states that schools must take action to prevent sexual harassment.

Another relevant law is Title IX of the Education Amendments of 1972. This act bans discrimination against students and employees on the basis of gender. It applies to any educational program receiving federal funds.

If you believe that you've been sexually harassed, report the incident to a school official. This person can be a teacher, administrator, or campus security officer. Check to see if your school has someone specially designated to handle your complaint, such as an affirmative action officer or Title IX coordinator.

You can also file a complaint with the Office of Civil Rights (OCR), a federal agency that makes sure schools comply with Title IX. In your complaint, include your name, address, and daytime phone number, along with the date of the incident and a description of it. Do this within 180 days of the incident. You can contact the OCR at 1-800-421-3481 or go to the agency's web site at **http://bcol01.ed.gov/CFAPPS/OCR/contact us.cfm**.

Your community and school might also offer resources to protect against sexual discrimination. Examples are public interest law firms, legal aid societies, and unions that employ lawyers to represent students.

Practice "netiquette"
Being *kind* while you're *online*

Netiquette is a collection of informal standards that apply to people who "talk" to each other through personal computers. Think of these standards as an etiquette code for the Internet.

Put out the flames.
"Flaming" takes place when someone sends an online message tinged with sarcasm or outright hostility. To create positive relationships when you're online, avoid sending such messages.

Some Internet users cut "flamers" a little slack. These users argue that an occasional outburst of anger is as appropriate when people are online as when they're face to face. But few advocate "flame wars"—a long series of insults and tirades exchanged among a few people. This kind of hostile dialogue can send the tone of an online community into the gutter.

Respect others' time and privacy.
People often turn to the Internet in the hope of saving time—not wasting it. You can accommodate their desires by typing concise messages. If you create your own web page, limit its download time by using simple, tasteful graphics. Update your page regularly and include your email address. Finally, if you have access to other people's computers, respect the privacy of their online documents.

Keep the medium in mind.
Communicating by computer eliminates nonverbal communication, including hand gestures and facial expressions. In face-to-face conversation, you rely on these subtle cues to decode another person's message. When your link to another person takes place only via words on a monitor, those cues vanish.

Use humor with caution. A joke that's funny when told in person might offend someone when written and sent via computer.

Use emoticons with care. Emoticons are combinations of keyboard characters that represent an emotion, such as :>). Emoticons are not appropriate for some communications, including exchanges with a prospective employer.

AVOID MESSAGES THAT APPEAR IN UPPERCASE LETTERS. They are the equivalent of shouting during a face-to-face conversation.

Remember—behind every computer is a person.
The cornerstone of netiquette is to remember that there is a human being on the receiving end of your communications. Whenever you're ready to send a message across the Internet, ask yourself one question: Would you say it to the person's face?

Effective email practices

In many workplace settings, email is as important as the telephone or fax machine. To get the most from this medium of communication, remember to:

Write an informative subject line. Along with your name, the subject line is what a recipient sees when your message shows up in his email box. Rather than writing a generic description, include a capsule summary of your message. "Report due next Tuesday" packs more information than "Report." If your message is urgent, include that word in the subject line as well.

Think short. Keep your subject line short, your paragraphs short, and your message as a whole short. Most people don't want to read long documents on a computer screen.

Provide context. If you're responding to a question from a previous email, quote that question in your response.

Minimize formatting. Many email programs don't display special formatting such as boldface, italics, and color. Stick to straight text.

Keep in mind that any message you send via the Internet is essentially a public document. Any competent hacker can intercept a private message. Before sending, ask yourself: What would be the costs if this information were made public?

Forget your career

Now that you've planned your career, forget it.

Forget your career for a few minutes—about the time it takes to read this article. This does not mean ignoring your future. In fact, it can actually breathe new life into your career plan.

When we're deep into details of planning, we can lose sight of the big picture. Listing skills, researching jobs, writing résumés, preparing for interviews—all these are useful. At the same time, attending to them can obscure our broadest goals.

Living a life is more than making a living. Before returning to the details of career planning, we can step back for a wide-angle view. We can ask: What is my basic purpose in life? How can I raise the quality of my life and be outrageously happy? What values do I want to support? What changes do I want to see in the world during my lifetime? What goods or services do I consider most valuable to the survival and well-being of the human race?

Each of these questions can reveal a life purpose. And once we're clear about the basic purpose of our lives, a wise career choice might just "fall out" of that discovery.

A purpose makes a career plan simpler and more powerful. With a purpose you can cut through stacks of job data, career-planning books, and employment statistics. Your life purpose is like the guidance system for a rocket: It keeps the plan on target while it reveals a path for soaring to the heights.

Your deepest desire may be to see that hungry children are fed, to make sure beautiful music keeps being heard, to help alcoholics become sober, to find a cure for AIDS, or simply to live a rewarding life. When that desire is clear, the smaller career decisions can be easier to make.

Career planning is really a series of choices. With a life purpose, we can handle those choices with ease. We can relate them to a single, overall goal. When faced with alternatives, we can hold them up to the single standard of a purpose.

Doing this offers the potential of fulfillment and joy. Focusing only on our own disappointments, needs, and problems can become limiting, even boring. When we adopt a purpose that goes beyond ourselves, our sense of limitation can fade into the background.

That's the power of a life purpose.

Sample life purposes

My purpose is to live, learn, love, and laugh.

My purpose is to have a wonderful life and to dramatically contribute to the quality of life on earth.

My purpose is to develop success strategies and ways to communicate those strategies.

I intend to become financially independent and raise happy, healthy children.

I will live in harmony with all creation.

I am here in this world to give and to receive.

My purpose is to be a healing presence in the world.

My purpose is to promote the well-being of my family.

In my life I seek to release suffering and serve others.

The purpose of my life is to become an accomplished pianist.

The purpose of my life is to live in a way that makes a difference for people and contributes to their happiness.

The purpose of my life is to serve.

The purpose of my life is to be loved and to be loving.

I aim to promote evolutionary change and be a catalyst for growth.

My purpose is to have a great time and laugh a lot.

EXERCISE

Write your life purpose

The *American Heritage Dictionary* defines the word *purpose* as:

1. The object toward which one strives or for which something exists; an aim or goal. . . . 2. A result or an effect that is intended or desired; an intention. . . . 3. Determination; resolution.

A life purpose is an overall direction, the most comprehensive statement of your aim in life.

Before you write your own purpose, keep in mind the difference between a goal and a life purpose. A goal can be fully achieved. A purpose is an overall direction that we can travel in for the rest of our lives without ever fully achieving it. A single purpose can generate many goals.

An effective purpose statement is highly practical. It tells us when our goals or behaviors are off-track. With our purpose firmly in mind, we can make moment-to-moment choices with real integrity.

Right now, spend five minutes drafting a one-sentence statement of your purpose in life. (It can be a long sentence!) Prompt yourself with questions based on the above definition:

- What am I striving for?
- What is the aim or goal of my life?
- What is the main result I want in my life? What am I determined or resolved to achieve with my life?

Another approach is to brainstorm endings to these sentences:

- In my lifetime, I want to be …
- In my lifetime, I want to do …
- In my lifetime, I want to have …
- The purpose of my life is to …

As you write, remember to focus on the purpose of *your* life—not of human life in general.

If you're not sure how to do all this—fine. You can revise your initial purpose statement later. For now, just pick up a pencil and write several drafts of your life purpose.

After the time is up, spend another 10 to 15 minutes revising your purpose statement.

To gain more insight and creative juice, do this exercise with a group and give everyone the option of sharing his or her purpose statement with the entire group.

Rewrite your purpose as many times as you like. It's also fine to brainstorm several different statements of your purpose. Later you might choose to combine these versions into one statement. In any case, rewrite your purpose to embody it in words that move you, that truly call you into action.

Finally, spend 5 to 15 minutes writing goals based on your purpose. Ask yourself: What would a person with this purpose do, have, and be?

Some goals for the year 10,000

Consider the following list of goals from one group of people who mentally stood in the year 10,000 and described what they saw:

We can decode natural communication systems. Now humans can communicate with rocks, plants, and all species of animals. The birds consistently tell us, "Don't worry. Be happy." (And when the birds talk, people listen.)

Physical pain is erased with thought.

War has been absent from the earth for centuries. Now conflict is resolved by teams of skilled negotiators who can be dispatched to any place on the planet in a matter of seconds—before any dispute can involve weapons.

Cities are limited in size to 100,000 people at most. This, combined with nonpolluting, clean, and safe mass transit, makes traffic congestion and vehicle accidents a thing of the distant past.

Natural disasters are predicted with absolute accuracy, far enough in advance to make mass evacuations possible. No longer is anyone killed because of tornadoes, floods, or earthquakes.

Prisons are eliminated, replaced by strictly supervised programs where people who commit crimes work to make amends to their victims.

Education at all levels—from kindergarten to postgraduate school—is universal and free.

EXERCISE

Create the next 10,000 years

As you plan your career, consider how a career fits into the whole expanse of your life. In fact, experiment with goals that go beyond your life span. Extend outward in time—as far as you can possibly imagine. There's no need to stop at setting goals for 10, 20, 50, or 100 years. Your goals can extend 500 . . . 1,000 . . . or even 10,000 years into the future.

If thinking this far into the future seems impossible or useless, keep a few things in mind:

- When viewing the entire span of human history, we often find that a decade, or even a century, is a relatively short period of time. Recall the history courses you took in school. There you probably considered entire decades in a matter of minutes. If we can talk about the distant past in this way, we can also talk about the distant future.

- Goals for the distant future represent highlights, not detailed agendas. When you set goals for he next decade or next century, you're plotting only the major events—the turning points in human affairs.

- When you think 500 years or more into the future, you go beyond your short-term self-interest. In 500 years you will be gone from the earth. So will any of your children, your grandchildren, and their grandchildren. With this long-range perspective, you can be more objective and consider the fate of humanity as a whole.

- After thinking in long stretches of time, you might find that the shorter stretches suddenly become easier. Once you've practiced thinking 100, 500, and even 10,000 years into the future, the notion of planning your next career can seem like child's play.

With the above points in mind, take the following steps:

1. Describe the world you want to see in the year 2500. Remember that this is not an exercise in predicting the world of 2500. Rather, make a statement about what you *want* humanity to achieve by that time.

2. After you've played with creating the world of 2500, go even farther out into the future. Conceive the world you'd like to see in the year 3000 or 5000.

3. Now stretch your planning muscles a little more and write goals for the year 10,000.

To fully experience the potential excitement of long, long-range planning, do this exercise with others. Working individually, spend 10 minutes writing on 3×5 cards. Record your goals for the year 2500. At the end of that time, ask all present to each share their goals with the group. Agree tolet anyone contribute a goal without criticism.

After you've completed this group exercise, list on 3×5 cards the goals that interest you the most. To get full benefit from this exercise, do it several times.

You don't have to believe in this concept of long, long-range goals. Just experiment with the idea and see if it has any usefulness for you.

_____
_____
_____
_____
_____
_____
_____
_____
_____
_____

Celebrate mistakes

When we plan a career or look for work, we inevitably make mistakes. Career planning is an art, not a science. There's no formula for the perfect career plan. There's no blueprint for the perfect résumé. And there's no way to assure a perfect job interview. Perfection is not a reasonable goal for career planning.

Even if we don't ask for perfection, we can achieve excellence. Excellence is compatible with making mistakes.

In fact, people who stretch themselves to meet worthy goals will sometimes miss. What makes them excel at career planning is the willingness to keep stretching—to learn from mistakes, adjust their plans, and begin again.

Because mistakes can teach us so much, they're priceless. Following are some reasons for celebrating mistakes, especially those that relate to finding a life's work.

- Mistakes in career planning show that we're taking risks instead of playing it safe. They're evidence that we're learning, expanding our skills, and aiming for wonderful lives.

- Celebrating our mistakes shows that we're recognizing them instead of hiding them. That greatly increases our chance to learn from mistakes.

- When we report out mistakes, we're more likely to get feedback from other people. That feedback can strengthen our career plans.

- Reporting our mistakes encourages others to talk about their mistakes. That can defuse our anxiety and sense of isolation.

- Mistakes help us stay on course by telling us when we're off course. We can then make appropriate corrections.

These ideas remind us that no one is perfect at this game called career planning. We're all in it together, just trying to do better. We need not hold the reins on our potential or fence in our spirits. We can choose, make mistakes, and choose again.

EXERCISE

Appreciate mistakes

Get together with a group of people interested in career planning and job hunting. Encourage everyone to talk freely about the mistakes made during this process. Promote humor and detachment by presenting awards for the "best" mistakes—those that hold the greatest potential for new learning.

Celebrate your plan— then begin again

Congratulations. You made it through this book. You probably read the text and completed many exercises, Discovery Statements, and Intention Statements. You had the opportunity to learn key steps in planning a career. And you are well on the way to a rich and satisfying work life. You deserve to party.

So party, see your favorite movie. Lie out in the grass for an afternoon and look up at the sky. Go on a picnic with people you love.

Then begin again.

The process of career planning never ends. We can return to it again and again. Career paths are best illustrated not with a straight line or a circle, but with a spiral. When we begin again, we may choose a new career. Or we may return to the same career choice with a deeper level of appreciation and understanding.

Either way, we remain open to the possibilities always unfolding in our lives. We invite ourselves to learn, change, and grow. All this can be done with grace and great ease. To help career planning work, begin again . . . and again . . .

and again. We can return time after time to our purposes, our dreams, and our wishes for a satisfying life.

Beginning again has led many people to colorful and distinguished careers. Elvis Presley started as a truck driver and became a singer. Albert Einstein was a clerk in a patent office before becoming a physicist. Anna Mary Moses, also known as Grandma Moses, was a housewife who began a career in painting at age 77. Kurt Vonnegut studied anthropology in college and then wrote novels. Scott Adams began his career as a bank teller before working at a major communications company in a technical job— where without any formal drawing experience he penned the first Dilbert cartoon, now syndicated in 2000 newspapers in 65 countries.

While working, we will gain many new insights into our values, passions, and life plans. This is a powerful process of self-discovery. In beginning again, we bring our plans to life.

Keep your career plan alive

You can use a variety of ways to remember your goals and continue creating your future, including your career. Following are some suggestions.

Display your goals

Without reminders, even skilled planners can forget their goals. One solution is to post written goals in prominent locations—the bathroom, bedroom, hall mirror, or office door. Also post goals on 3x5 cards and tape them to walls or store them next to your bed. Review the cards every night and every morning.

You can make your goals even more visible. Create an elaborate poster, sign, advertisement, or collage that displays your life purpose. Use frames, color, graphics, and other visual devices to rivet your attention on your goals.

Write goals daily

Grab a few precious minutes here and there to write and revise goals. In sixty seconds or less you can jot down a goal or two. You can also set your wristwatch alarm for a certain time each day and take five minutes to write goals. Reread your purpose statement or revise your career goals while taking a break at work.

Add to your plan

Goals have a way of occurring to us at the oddest moments—while we're waiting in line, riding the bus, or negotiating rush hour traffic. With a little advance planning, you can capture the goals that pop into your mind at these times. One option is to carry a few 3x5 cards and a pen in your pocket or purse. As the advertisement said, don't leave home without them. Or pack a small tape recorder with you. Speak your goals and preserve them for the ages.

Advertise your career plan

Everyone you know is a possible ally in achieving your goals. Take a tip from Madison Avenue and advertise. Tell everyone you meet about what you plan to be, do, or have. Make your career plan public.

Enlist others to support your plan

Family members and close friends might balk at some of your goals: "You want to promote world peace. That's crazy! It will never happen. Why waste your time?" If you encounter such responses, remember that there are ways to work with resistance.

One strategy is to ask directly for support. Explain how much the goal means to you and what you'll do to achieve it. Mention that you're willing to alter the goal as circumstances change. In some cases, this might be all that's needed to win over your loved ones.

An option related to this strategy is to *keep* talking about your vision of the future. Goals that sound outlandish to your family at first might become easier for them to accept over time.

Schedule time for career planning

When it comes to creating the future, you'll probably hear people say, "Yeah, that sounds like a good idea. I'll get around to it some day." Yet the long-awaited day might never come. Some people go to their graves without a long-range goal.

To avoid this fate, schedule a specific time and place to set and review goals. Make this a regular appointment with yourself, and treat it as seriously as an appointment with your doctor.

Teach career planning

There's a saying: We teach what we most want to learn. You can make this idea an incentive for creating the future. Explain career planning to your friends and family members. Volunteer to lead a seminar, workshop, or community education class on this topic. If you have children, assist them in setting goals. Ask them to speak often about their future, and listen with full attention to what they say.

Work with a coach

Perhaps a skilled planner would be willing to become your mentor. It pays to ask, and such a person might feel flattered if you do. You can even hire a coach for goal setting and achievement, much as some people hire a personal trainer for help with exercise.

Enjoy the rewards

Savor the feeling that comes with crossing items off your to-do list, or with moving your goal cards from the "to do" stack to the "done" stack. You might wish to save the cards filled with the goals you've completed; that way you can celebrate your achievements. Or give those cards to others and suggest that they adopt one of your completed goals.

Take action on your goals

Let the thrill of meeting a goal lead you to setting more goals. Break large goals into small tasks that you can complete in one hour or less. Experience feelings of accomplishment often.

JOURNAL ENTRY

Intention Statement

Consider setting aside a time to work through all or part of this book again. Then set a deadline for doing so. Complete the following sentence by including specific dates:

I intend to repeat the planning process outlined in this book starting on _____/_____/_____ and ending on _____/_____/_____.

JOURNAL ENTRY

Discovery/Intention Statement

You've done a lot of writing while going through this book. To retain the key insights from this process, look over your responses to the exercises, Discovery Statements, and Intention Statements. Summarize below your key discoveries about career planning. List any Intention Statements that call for further action. Write any new Intention Statements that seem appropriate.

_____

_____

_____

_____

_____

_____

_____

_____

_____

_____

_____

Name _____ Date _____/_____/_____

 1 Why is it important to understand styles in the workplace?

2 What is the importance of seeing the workplace as a laboratory for learning from experience?

3 What is the most important way to promote cross-cultural understanding? Explain your answer.

4 Describe at least two benefits of creating goals for the year 2500 and beyond.

5 List five ways to keep your career plan alive.

Suggested Reading

Using this book can immerse you in the process of career planning. Other materials can provide further details in specific areas.

Career planning is a vast subject. People working in this area have discovered many tools for achieving fulfilling careers and rewarding lives. Many of their suggestions could work for you. Following are some recommended print materials. Using them will lead you to others.

 Visit Houghton Mifflin's Career Planning web site for additional web resources to gain further information about career planning: http://collegesurvival.college.hmco.com/students.

Bock, Jay A., et. al. *101 Best Resumes and Cover Letters*. New York: McGraw-Hill, 2001.

Bolles, Richard N. *What Color Is Your Parachute? A Practical Manual for Job-Hunters and Career-Changers.* Berkeley, CA: Ten Speed Press. Revised annually.

Bridges, William. *JobShift: How to Prosper in a Workplace Without Jobs*. Reading, MA: Addison-Wesley, 1994.

Criscito, Pat. *Resumes in Cyberspace.* New York: Barron's Educational Series, 2000.

Ellis, Dave. *Becoming a Master Student,* 10th ed. Boston: Houghton Mifflin, 2003.

Ellis, Dave. *Falling Awake.* Rapid City, SD: Breakthrough Enterprises, 2001.

Ellis, Dave. *Creating Your Future: Five Steps to the Life of Your Dreams.* Boston: Houghton Mifflin, 1998.

Ellis, Dave, and Stan Lankowitz. *Human Being: A Manual for Happiness, Health, Love, and Wealth.* Rapid City, SD: Breakthrough Enterprises, 1995.

Enelow, Wendy S., and Louise Kursmark. *Expert Resumes for Computer and Web Jobs.* Indianapolis: JIST Works, 2001.

Gale, Linda, and Barry Gale. *Discover What You're Best At: A Complete Career System That Lets You Test Yourself to Discover Your Own True Career Abilities.* New York: Simon & Schuster, 1998.

Greene, Susan D., and Melanie C. L. Martel. *The Ultimate Job Hunter's Guidebook.* Boston: Houghton Mifflin, 2001.

Hagberg, Janet, and Richard Leider. *The Inventurers: Excursions in Life and Career Renewal.* Reading, MA: Addison-Wesley, 1998.

Kastre, Michael F., Nydia Rodriguez Kastre, and Alfred G. Edwards. *The Minority Career Guide: What African Americans, Hispanics, and Asian Americans Must Know to Succeed in Corporate America.* Princeton, NJ: Peterson's, 1993.

Kolin, Philip C. *Successful Writing at Work.* Boston: Houghton Mifflin, 2001.

Murdick, William, and Jonathan C. Bloemker. *The Portable Technical Writer.* Boston: Houghton Mifflin, 2001.

Murdick, William. *The Portable Business Writer.* Boston: Houghton Mifflin, 1999.

Ober, Scot. *Contemporary Business Communication.* Boston: Houghton Mifflin, 2003.

Tieger, Paul, et al. *Do What You Are: Discover the Perfect Career for You Through the Secrets of Personality Type.* New York: Brown and Company, 2001.

Winter, Barbara. *Making a Living Without a Job.* New York: Bantam Books, 1993.

Yate, Martin John. *Knock'em Dead 2001: The Ultimate Job Seekers Sources with Great Answers to 200 Tough Questions.* New York: Adams Media Company, 2001.

PHOTO AND ILLUSTRATION CREDITS

Alamy: page 108;

© Keith Brofsky/PhotoDisc/ PictureQuest: page 45;

Mark Cass/PictureQuest: pages 52, 106, 107;

Ron Chapple/PictureQuest: pages v, vi, x, 24, 108;

Steve Cole/PictureQuest: page 53;

Comstock: page 63;

Corbis/Royalty Free: page 70;

Creatas/PictureQuest: page 33t;

EyeWire: page 89;

The Fuller Projection Map design is a trademark of the Buckminster Fuller Institute ©1938, 1967 & 1992. All rights reserved: page 43;

Walter Kopec: page 59;

Brian Jude Reardon: page 1

Ryan McVay/Getty Images: page v, viii, x, 102;

Ryan McVay/PhotoDisc: page v, vi, x, 42;

PhotoDisc © 2002: pages 10, 14, 20, 25, 57, 88br, 114, 116, 117, 118;

PictureQuest: pages v, vii, x, 6, 17, 46, 50, 66, 74, 82;

Philip & Karen Smith/Getty Images: page 47;

Superstock: pages 49, 106, 107;

Wonderfile: pages 33bl, 33br, 34t, 34m, 34b, 87tl, 87br, 88l, 88tr, 97.

INDEX

A

Abstract conceptualization learning stage, 29
Accommodators learning style, 29
Accountability, 27
Achievements, 35, 83–84, 108, 119
Active experimentation learning stage, 29
America's Job Bank database, 46
Aristotle, 102
Assets, 39–40
Assimilators learning style, 29
Associations, professional, 60

B

Behavioral preferences, 103–104
Bolles, Richard, *What Color Is Your Parachute?*, 46
Boren, David, 82
Bowen, Elizabeth, 42
Budget, creating, 70–71
Businesses, creating, 84

C

California Psychological Inventory, 36
Candidness, 27
Career Ability Placement Survey (CAPS), 36
Career changes, mid-life, 17
Career information
    building structure of, 63
    computer based, 45–46
Career opportunities of employers, 59
Career planning
    benefits of, 10, 12–13, 15, 68
    choices, 10, 11, 63, 116
    commitment to, 15
    condition of survival, 52
    dreams, 10
    elements of, 2
    ideas, 13
    Internet usage, 46
    life purposes, 112–113
    mistakes in, 116
    negative thoughts, 12, 14
    online resources of, 59
    process of, 14, 15, 118–119
    scheduling time for, 118
    teaching, 119
    web sites, 2, 15, 30, 36
Career plans
    advertising, 118
    discovery/intention statement, 7
    explanation of, 5
    formats, 78–79
    laid off, 54
    revisions of, 76
    updating, 118
    writing, 7

Career Resource Center, 46
Career resources, web sites, 46, 72
Career Thoughts Inventory, 36
Careers
    choices in, 80
    definition of, 7
    expanding choices of, 43
    ideas for, 44
    lists of, 9
    options for, 83
    recommendations for, 11
Chat rooms, 56
Civil Rights Act of 1964, Title VII
    ban of discrimination, 108
    guidelines for interpreting, 110
Commitment, 15
Common goals, strategies for, 106
Communications
    commonality in cultures, 107–108
    Internet dialogue, 111
    nonverbal dialogue, 111
Company annual reports on Internet, 59
Competencies, core of success, 37
Computer resources
    for career information, 45–46
    See also Internet
Computer skills, training for, 54
Computers
    selection needs, 55
    web research, 57–58
Concrete experience learning stage, 29
Conflict, resolving, 104
Content skills, 33
Convergers, learning style, 29
Conversation space
    balance of, 21
    definition of, 20
Course catalog, 32
Cover letters, 94–96
Coworkers, success with, 103–104
Creation, planning by, 70–71
Creativity, 73, 77
Credibility, web sites, 61
Cultures
    corporate, 108
    differences in, 106–107
    ethnocentrism of, 108
Curie, Marie, 42
Cyberspace updates
    web site, 56

D

De Bono, Edward, 66
Detachment, 27
Dictionary of Occupational Titles, 46
Discovery statement, career plan, 7–9

Discovery/intention statement, sexism
    revealed by, 110
Discrimination
    community protection, 110
    proof of, 108
    sexual harassment, 109
Divergers learning style, 29
Diversifications, 84
Diversities, 106
Domain goals, 75
Dreams, exploration of, 17
Dyer, Wayne, 82

E

Education, 53
Education Amendments of 1972, Title IX
    bans discrimination against students, 110
    See also Discrimination
Email
    free, 56
    guidelines for, 111
    public document warning, 111
Employers
    information interviews, 47
    Web home page, 59
    Web research, 59
Employment security, 52–54
Equal Employment Opportunity Commission
    (EEOC), 108
Eureka Skills Inventory, 36
Expanding, definition of, 2

F

FedWorld, U.S. government job openings on, 46
Financial resources, 39
Foundations for skills of success, 37
Future, creating, 21, 115

G

Gandhi, Mohandas, 6
Goals
    accomplishing, 119
    categories, 75
    common, strategies for, 106
    for the future, 22, 73, 114
    formats, 78
    paths to, 74
    reminders of, 118
    short and long term, 7–8
    support for, 118
Government publications, resources of, 46
Graduate school programs, 60

H

Hall Occupational Orientation Inventory
    (HOOI), 36

Hunt, Diana Scharf, 66
Hyperlinks, definition of, 56, 57

I

Ideal life, 18
Ideas, career planning, 5
Intention statement, career plan, 7, 9
Internet
    accessing, 56
    career planning, 46
    company annual reports, 59
    critical thinking, 61
    directories, 57
    file transfer, 56
    job hunting, 59
    search engines, 57
    trends, 60
    usage, web sites, 46
    validity of, 62
Internet service provider (ISP), 56
Internships
    hands-on research, 50
    work experience, 48–49
Interpersonal skills, 37
Interviews
    follow up procedures, 100
    preparation for, 97
    strategies for, 98–99
    structure of, 47, 48
Involvement, 27

J

Job database, web sites, 46
Job fields, defining, 63
Job hunting
    Internet, 59
    rehearsal of, 85
    strategies, 83–84
    teams, 87
Job security, 52
Jobs
    changes, 52–53
    definition, 7
    history of, 52–53
    loss of, 54
    See also Careers

L

Languages
    gender-fair, 5
    multicultural differences, 107
    nonverbal, 103
Lathrop, Richard, x
Lay-offs, planning for, 54
Learning styles
    definition, 29
    developing, 30
    resources on, 30
    web site, 29

Learning, stages of, 29
Life purpose, 112–113
Lorde, Audre, 24
Love, 27

M

Microtasks, 84
Mid-life career changes, 17
Mistakes, 116
Money management, 54
Multicultural workplace, 106–108
    See also Cultures
Myers-Briggs Type Indicator (MBTI), 36

N

Narrowing down, definition of, 2
Negermajian, Katherine, 24
Netiquette, Internet etiquette code, 111
Networking
    annual meetings, 60
    job opportunities, 48, 88
    online groups, 60
    strategies, 87–88
    use of, 110
    with cultures, 108

O

Observational preferences, 103–104
Occupational Outlook Handbook, 46
Office of Civil Rights (OCR), filing complaint
    with, 110
Online resources, job hunting using, 59
Online services, accessing, 56

P

Past
    dominance of, 21
    focus on, 20
Performance evaluations, 108
Personal Career Development Profile (PCDP),
    36
Placement offices, graduate schools, 60
Planning
    by creation, 70–71
    freedom in life, 67–68
    types of, 70
Possibilities, 27
Present
    dominance of, 21
    focus on, 20
Priorities, 74, 79
Procrastination, ending, 69
Promotiveness, 27

Q

quid pro quo harassment, definition of, 109

R

Rank ordering, 74
Rankin, Diana, 6

Reflective observation, learning stage, 29
Research
    group interviews, 48
    information interviews, 47
    Internet methods, 57–58
    job techniques, 47–49
    volunteering, 48
Resources
    government publications, 46
    Internet, 59
    list of, 45
    trends, 60
Résumés
    building and posting, 59, 60
    cover letters, 94–96
    examples on web site, 91
    samples, 91–93
    scannable, 90
    strategies for, 89–90
Ride, Sally, x
Roosevelt, Theodore, 102

S

SCANS reports See Secretary's Commission on
    Achieving Necessary Skills
Schedule, daily, 31
SDS See Self-Directed Search
Search engines for career groups, 60
Secretary's Commission on Achieving
    Necessary Skills (SCANS)
    foundations and competencies, 37
    report on the web site, 37
Self-Directed Search (SDS), 36
Self-discovery
    assets, 39–40
    beginning again through, 73, 117
    personal qualities, 25
    vocational assessments, 36
Self-employment, 17
Self-generation, 27
Sexism, strategies to combat, 109–110
Sexual harassment
    definition of, 109
    filing complaint web sites, 110
    reporting of, 110
    verbal and physical behavior of, 109
Skills
    basic, 37
    computer, 54
    definition of, 33
    future value of, 38
    importance of, 53
    personal qualities, 37
    problem solvers, 89–90
    recognition of, 34
    thinking, 37
    types of, 33, 34
    used for achievements, 35
Stress. management of, 54
Strong Interest Inventory, 36

Success, definition of, 19
Success, foundations and competencies for, 37
Support team, 86

T

Technophobia, overcoming, 56
Telecommute, 53
Thank you notes, 100
Time management, 84
Timelines, 71, 74, 78
Transferable skills
  definition, 33
  examples of, 34
Trends, 60
Turner, Dr. Dale E., 24

U

U.S. government, job openings in, 46
Unemployment, 54
Universal Resource Locator (URL), usage of, 57
Usenet (newsgroups), 56

V

Values
  clarification of, 26
  definition of specific, 27
Vocational assessments, list of, 36
Vocational Preference Inventory (VPI), 36
Volunteers
  organizations web sites, 48
  work, 48

W

What Color Is Your Parachute?, Bolles, Richard, 46
Women in Communications, 110
Work projects, 104
Workforce, comparison of, 62
Workplace styles, 103–104
World Wide Web (WWW)
  career planning pages, 59
  definition, 56

Z

Zero-based budgeting, 71

Monday	Tuesday	Wednesday	Thursday	Friday	Saturday	Sunday

Name _____

Month _____

Name ———

Month ———

Monday	Tuesday	Wednesday	Thursday	Friday	Saturday	Sunday

Monday	Tuesday	Wednesday	Thursday	Friday	Saturday	Sunday

Name _____

Month _____

Name ———

Month ———

Monday				
Tuesday				
Wednesday				
Thursday				
Friday				
Saturday				
Sunday				

Monday	Tuesday	Wednesday	Thursday	Friday	Saturday	Sunday

Name —————————— Month ——————————

Name ———————

Month ———————

Monday	Tuesday	Wednesday	Thursday	Friday	Saturday	Sunday

Monday	Tuesday	Wednesday	Thursday	Friday	Saturday	Sunday

Name _____   Month _____

Name ——————

Month ——————

Monday	Tuesday	Wednesday	Thursday	Friday	Saturday	Sunday